ALCATRAZ ISLAND
MAXIMUM SECURITY

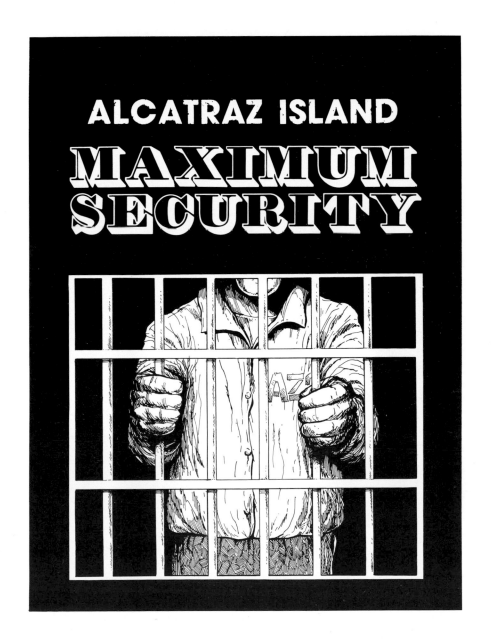

by

Donald J. Hurley

FOG BELL
ENTERPRISES

Other books by Donald J. Hurley:

ALCATRAZ ISLAND MEMORIES, ©1987

All inquiries to:

Fog Bell Enterprises
P.O. Box 1376
Sonoma, CA 95476

Printed in the United States of America

First Edition —Second Printing, April 1991

Library of Congress Catalogue Number # 89-80985
ISBN # 0-9620546-1-5

Cover Illustration by Tom Hunnicut
Cover Design by Jim Koegler
Edited by Mary A. Coverdale-Roberts, M.A.
Typesetting by Esther L. Harris
Typography and Layout by James M. Harris—Harris Graphic Design
Printing by Barlow Printing, Inc.

BARLOW
PRINTING
INCORPORATED

409 First Street, Petaluma, CA 94952

ACKNOWLEDGMENTS

This book could have been written and published only with the assistance of the following people and organizations:

- The staffs of the Golden Gate National Recreation Area; The National Maritime Museum, San Francisco; and the Golden Gate National Park Association.
- Rich Weideman, Supervisory Park Ranger, Bay District; and the Alcatraz Island Supervisory Ranger Staff.
- All the dedicated National Park Service Rangers who serve on Alcatraz Island and relate its colorful history each day to visitors.
- The Alcatraz Alumni Association, which was founded in 1965. An abundance of the information contained in this book came about as a result of conversations the writer had with several member officers. The association, of which the author was president, consists of former officers and their families who worked and lived on "The Rock." Sadly, it is a dwindling number as there are no third-generation direct ties with the penitentiary. At the annual meeting and picnic, interviews with these former officers help to assure a near-accurate account of the lore of Alcatraz. An interested reader can therefore be provided the ability to experience this small slice of history from eye-witness accounts.
- Charles G. Hurley Sr., Senior Correctional Officer/Instructor (In Memory of) who served at Alcatraz 1942-1953. Written material (journal) and conversations over a period of several years.

PHOTOGRAPHS:

Pacific Aerial Surveys
Associated Press
Golden Gate National Recreation Area
National Maritime Museum, San Francisco
Edward Faulk
John "Bud" Hart
United States Department of Justice
Federal Bureau of Prisons—Photographic Archives
Lee and Maxine Bowman (Lieutenant Frank Johnson collection)
San Francisco Public Library
Bruce Badzik—Pelican Island Photographic Service (Alcatraz landscapes)

The author acknowledges the artistic ability of those whose photographs appear in this book anonymously. Original sources of some photographs could not be obtained.

SPECIAL THANKS TO:

Philip Bergen, Associate Warden, Ret., served at Alcatraz 1939-1955.
John Roberts, Federal Bureau of Prisons (Chief Archivist)
Charles G. Hurley Jr., the author's brother, for allowing the author to use excerpts from their father's journal.
Nick Baxter (fictitious name), ex-inmate of Alcatraz interviewed November 1988 in Los Angeles County.
Jim Koegler, an enthusiastic friend.
J.B.
W.C.
A.B.

This book is dedicated to my wife,
Gwen.
Her patience seemed to know no bounds
while I labored over this book.
For that I will always be grateful.

FOREWORD

Don Hurley actually lived a part of the Alcatraz experience. His father, Charles G. Hurley, was employed as a federal correctional officer for almost 30 years, the last 11 years having been spent at Alcatraz Island. Don took up residence on Alcatraz with his family in 1942 at the age of seven. Included in the family were his mother and nine-year-old brother. He grew to manhood within the shadows of the most famous of all the United States penitentiaries. After his father retired from federal prison service, Don left Alcatraz Island to pursue a career of his own.

This, however, is not an account of family life on Alcatraz Island. The book deals in an accurate and positive manner with America's toughest penitentiary and the men on both sides of the bars who served time there. It is an account of how some inmates coped well with "The Rock" and of those who did not.

Through a combination of written narrative and photographs, the author takes his readers on a journey that delves beneath the mystique of Alcatraz Island. The book gives each of its readers a front row seat to view why this 12-acre island in San Francisco Bay was designated the nation's only ultramaximum- security penitentiary.

The telling of this story was made possible through in-depth research, verbal, and written recollections of the author's father, as well as interviews with some of the officers who worked on "The Rock" and inmates who served time there. There is also the author's 11-year experience of living on Alcatraz Island.

John "Bud" Hart
Alcatraz Island
1948-1962
Member
Alcatraz Alumni Association

ALCATRAZ ISLAND
FEDERAL PENITENTIARY

1934 – 1963

INTRODUCTION

Alcatraz Island has had a long and illustrious history. In 1850 the island was occupied by the United States Army Engineers. The army was commissioned to establish a fortress on the island in order to protect settlers in the San Francisco Bay Area. By 1850 hundreds of people were arriving each month by ship enroute to the recently discovered gold fields in search of fame and fortune.

Alcatraz was first noted by the Spanish in 1769 and named in 1775 by a Spanish captain. However, it was not until California became a state that this rocky little island with its steep cliffs stepped onto the pages of history.

The U.S. Army occupation of Alcatraz continued for 84 years. From 1850 through the turn of the century, the island functioned mainly as a fortress. However, as the twentieth century dawned, it became apparent that the Post of Alcatraz Island had irreversibly blossomed into a full-blown military prison. It would continue in that capacity until the end of the island's military days in 1934.

Alcatraz next went through its most famous phase beginning in 1934 when it became America's first ultra-maximum-security penitentiary. During its 29-year history as a federal prison, "The Rock" housed some of the most notorious criminals this country has ever produced.

Donald J. Hurley, © 1989.
Alcatraz Island 1942-1953.

Next Page Overleaf: The prison yard looking north

CONTENTS

ALCATRAZ ELUDES DISCOVERY
Nesting Pelicans Give Island Its Name

Juan Cabrillo discovered California in 1542. After claiming all the land touched by the Pacific Ocean in the name of Spain, Cabrillo pointed his galleon north to see where this coastline would take him. After sailing past the entrance to the largest natural harbor in the world, later to be known as the Golden Gate, the entrance to San Francisco Bay, Cabrillo turned south and retraced his steps to the Channel Islands, approximately 25 miles off the Southern California coast. Cabrillo died there of an arm infection and was buried on one of the islands by his crew.

Several years later, Sir Francis Drake also sailed past the entrance to San Francisco Bay without noticing it. Two explanations are put forth to help explain the missed sightings. First, both Cabrillo and Drake may have sailed to the west of the Farallones Islands because of shallow water or reefs. Second, the presence of fog, not unusual for this area, may have obstructed the view of the harbor. As it turned out, San Francisco Harbor was not discovered for another 200 years as a result of a land expedition.

In early September 1769, Gaspar de Portola, the military governor of Upper California, set out with an expeditionary force which headed north from San Diego. Its purpose was to find a land route to Monterey Bay. The bay had been discovered from the sea during the sixteenth century but had never been reached by land.

After several unsuccessful attempts to locate the bay, Portola decided to send out two smaller expeditions. One of the expeditions was under the command of Sgt. Ortega. He led his men due north and was rewarded after several days when his party climbed to the top of a hill which overlooks San Francisco Bay. Even though the party had missed Monterey, they did discover a huge natural harbor. Although Ortega must have seen Alcatraz Island, it was not named until six years later.

Opposite Page: Portola and his party overlook San Francisco Bay – 1769

In 1775 Captain Ayala sailed into San Francisco Bay with orders from the Spanish government to inspect the harbor. Ayala made a notation in his ship's log that a small rocky island in the bay had no suitable anchorage or shelter for ships. He further noted the island had hundreds of nesting pelicans, and so he named it "Isla De Los Alcatraces," which translates to "Island of the Pelicans." The pelicans remained in peaceful bliss for another 75 years until 1850 when California became a state.

Above: Spanish Captain Ayala enters San Francisco – 1775

Alcatraz Island: Maximum Security

ALCATRAZ SERVES STRATEGIC MILITARY AIMS

Soldiers Join Pelicans, Transform Island Into Fort

Shortly after California became a state, U.S. Army Engineers began the construction of a fortress on Alcatraz to protect the influx of settlers to the area. After the discovery of gold in California, the United States government felt that a foreign power, possibly Mexico, might entertain the thought of retaking the entire area. Therefore, Alcatraz was to be one of three fortresses to be built near the en-

Left: First permanent lighthouse on the west coast, 1854, alongside taller one completed in 1909

trance to San Francisco Bay.

Actual construction began in 1853 and was completed and ready for troops in 1859. The new fortress was designated the Post of Alcatraz; however, most of those who served there called it Fort Alcatraz.

With its completion in 1859, the Post of Alcatraz become the first permanent fortress on the west coast.

Foghorns and Lighthouse Make Isle Into a Beacon

There was a plan to build a lighthouse at the same time the fortress plans were put forth. The lighthouse was completed in 1854 and became operational that same year. Like the fortress, the lighthouse became the first on the west coast. It was in operation for 55 years before it was replaced by a newer and more efficient one in 1909. This new lighthouse was maintained by a resident staff member of the U.S. Coast Guard until the federal prison closed in 1963. At that time it was put on fully automatic operation. In 1970 the Coast Guard residential quarters were gutted by fire; however, the tower itself survived and to this day still guides ships around its rocky shores.

One concern the army encountered early in its occupation of Alcatraz Island was the problem of thick drifting fog on the bay. The army decided that something was needed to warn ships that plowed somewhat blindly through the harbor during the foggy days and nights. So in 1857 the army erected a half-ton fog bell. It sounded when the bell was struck by a heavy metal ball attached to an iron rod. The bell worked on a pulley system, which had to be wound by hand and required one man approximately an hour to wind. Two larger fog bells were constructed on the island in 1871 and 1877. They were built over the water for greatest sound distance. Although the fog bells were less than an ideal system, they did manage on more than one occasion to avert ships from running aground on Alcatraz.

During the 11 years that the author lived on Alcatraz island, two modern foghorns were in place, one at the extreme northern tip of the island and the other near the southwestern end. Both foghorns, as well as the lighthouse, are maintained by the U.S. Coast Guard. Today all three systems are in use and are fully automated.

Top: 1857 fog bell – note size of bell and pulley system.

Left: Alcatraz in the late 1800s

Alcatraz Reveals Its True Nature—A Prison

Early in the development of Alcatraz by army engineers, it seemed almost inevitable that the island fortress would evolve into a military prison. Less than a decade after construction began on the fortress, the army was temporarily housing military prisoners from the San Francisco Presidio for various minor offenses. It caused somewhat of a hardship to lodge prisoners on the island as the Post of Alcatraz was designed strictly as a fortress. A small wooden building had to be constructed for a prison compound. Army personnel were shifted from artillery duty to guard the prisoners. This move left some of the gun posts undermanned. By the middle of the 1860s, the army stockade was bulging with more than 100 prisoners, which necessitated the construction of a much larger brick building to accommodate the growing prisoner population.

Army records reflect that during the 1870s the Post of Alcatraz had more than 400 military prisoners incarcerated at the fortress. The United States Army continued to build a larger prison compound, but by 1880 it was plain to see that the army was beginning to change its priorities; the Post of Alcatraz was in reality now a military prison instead of a fortress.

In 1907 the U.S. War Department decided to build a permanent military prison. Construction began almost at once; however, it was not completed until 1912. Some of the work was completed by army prisoners themselves, and some of them became the first to be housed in the new facility.

Right: Construction of the cell house about 1908

The Post of Alcatraz was about to enter its final phase. In 1915 the military prison officially became the military disciplinary barracks, an army rehabilitation center for training. It would continue in that capacity for the next 19 years.

There were a number of support buildings constructed by the army during its tenure as a fortress and then as a military prison. Many of these buildings remained in use by the Federal Bureau of Prisons until "The Rock" closed in 1963. An example of army construction on the island is 64 Building, which is a three-story structure that overlooks the dock. The building was built in 1905 to house military guards and their families. The author had an uncle who served as a military guard during the 1920s and lived in this building. This same building also served as the author's first residence after moving to Alcatraz in 1942 at age seven.

The island and its variety of structures offer an impressive sight to tourists stepping off the daily tour boats.

*Above: Alcatraz about the time it
became a federal prison – 1934*

Right: Early cell block – note bridges

GANGSTERS MAKE ALCATRAZ THEIR HOME
Justice Department Builds Ultramaximum-Security Prison

By the beginning of the 1930s, the military prisoner population on Alcatraz was in a sharp decline. The Department of Justice, however, was having its problems as the gangster era was at its peak. Justice officials felt that convicting gangsters and sending them to existing federal prisons did very little good. The reason for this was that the big-time gangsters, like Alfonse "Scarface" Capone, lived just about as well in prison as they did on the outside. It was decided, therefore, that a new type of prison would be opened.

The new prison would be America's first ultramaximum-security penitentiary and would have to meet certain specifications. First, officials needed a place that was somewhat isolated. Second, they wanted a no-nonsense warden; and third, they felt that they needed correctional officers that had had experience at other federal facilities. The Department of Justice turned the project over to its newly formed arm, the Bureau of Prisons. The final decision was made. Alcatraz Island would be the ideal location. There was already a prison in operation, and with upgrading, it could be virtually escape-proof. The only problem was that local officials of the San Francisco Bay Area were not happy with the prospect of having some of this country's most notorious gangsters imprisoned practically on their doorstep.

The Bureau of Prisons, however, had made up its mind. With the hiring of one of the most respected wardens in the country, James A. Johnston, the bureau was ready to make the transition from army prison to federal prison.

Warden Johnston would hold the position of warden on "The Rock" for the first 14 years of its 29-year operation. He would personally supervise the entire upgrading of the old army prison.

Every bit of modern technology was used in an attempt to make this new ultramaximum-security facility escape-proof. For example, full-body metal detectors were installed at key points throughout the prison to cut down on the movement of contraband.

Flat army bars were replaced with cutproof round ones. The entire prison building was reinforced. Gun ports and gun cages were installed along with new, stronger security doors. These were just a few of the changes that were made in order to house the notorious inmates that were to take up residence here. When Warden Johnston was finished, the prison had undergone a complete face-lift.

Because Warden Johnston knew that San Francisco Bay Area officials were skeptical of having so many infamous criminals housed on Alcatraz, he gave them several detailed tours of "The Rock" in order to minimize their fears of possible escapes.

At last the big day arrived, and the federal penitentiary at Alcatraz was opened for business on August 11, 1934.

The first group of inmates to arrive at Alcatraz were transferred from the federal prison at McNeil Island, Washington. Warden Johnston also inherited 32 military prisoners when the army turned over the prison to the Justice Department. The next 50+ inmates arrived by a special train from Atlanta Federal Prison. The transfer, which was kept secret, left Atlanta in three special window-barred Pullman coaches. The train proceeded to the city of Tiburon, which is at the north end of San Francisco Bay. The Pullman cars were then rolled directly onto a train barge. Under a tug's power, it floated to Alcatraz Island with its notorious cargo. One of the inmates on board this special train was none other than Capone.

Left: Warden Johnston showing Bay Area officials the prison

Bottom: Special train arriving from Atlanta Federal Prison at Alcatraz with more than 50 inmates in 1934

It was obvious from the day Alcatraz opened that here was going to be an unusual way in which notorious inmates were to be handled by the federal prison system. Inmate population would rarely exceed 280 at any one time. There would be only one inmate to a cell, which measured nine feet long by five feet wide. One-man cells remained enforced for the entire 29 years Alcatraz operated as a federal prison. The officials' objective was not to rehabilitate the inmate but to make him conform to rules and regulations. Warden Johnston also personally picked the officers who were going to work at this place called "The Rock." When he was finished, there were approximately 90 correctional officers in place. This was a ratio of one officer for every 3.1 inmates, the highest officer-to-inmate ratio in the entire federal prison system.

There were other conditions set down for this new kind of maximum security experiment called Alcatraz Federal Penitentiary. There would be no federal court commitments sent directly to Alcatraz. Only a few exceptions to this policy occurred during the prison's 29-year history. If an inmate became too much trouble at another federal prison, he would be transferred to Alcatraz. An inmate would not be paroled from Alcatraz. He would be transferred to another federal prison prior to release. This was done so that a parolee would not have direct access to the press in San Francisco, who were always eager for any news coming out of the prison. With the rules and regulations set down, Warden Johnston and his staff were ready to get down to business at hand—watching over society's hardest criminals.

OTHER PRISONS SEND THEIR WORST OFFENDERS TO ALCATRAZ

Inmates Promised Transfers for Good Behavior

Life started out for all inmates on "The Rock" under the premise that they were to serve their sentences and nothing more. They were told that if they kept their noses clean and stayed out of trouble, inmates could, in most cases, expect to be transferred to a less restrictive federal prison within three to five years to serve the remainder of their sentences.

When the prison opened it appeared that all the convicted gangsters in the country were ending up at Alcatraz. In later years, as the gangster era came to a close in the late 1930s, inmates were being sent to Alcatraz for other reasons, such as bank robbery, murder (under federal statute), and a host of other federal crimes. The policy, however, that inmates would be sent to Alcatraz only if they became incorrigible in other federal prisons remained enforced.

PRISONERS WORK TO FEND OFF BOREDOM

Jobs Available in Maintenance, Laundry

Warden Johnston made the inmates earn their jobs in the various workshops, such as the mat shop, the brush shop, the furniture shop, or laundry. The opportunity to work was earned by conforming to the rules and regulations. In the beginning when the inmates earned their jobs, they were allowed more yard time. Most inmates were locked in their cells for about 13 hours each day, so any time away from their cells was a welcome change.

The new laundry building was completed prior to World War II, and right from the beginning of the war it became a very busy place. As it was the largest federal

Right: Northwest end of island showing industry complex. The long building to the right is the laundry.

Below: Prison tailor shop

Opposite Page: Inmates returning from workshops to the cell house by way of the prison yard.

laundry facility in the Bay Area, several military installations used its service. They included Fort Mason, The Sixth Army Presidio, Fort McDowell, and of course, the dependents who resided on the island.

By 1942 Warden Johnston had implemented his "work for pay" program, which allowed inmates to receive compensation for their labor. Compensation was figured on skill levels rated from one to four. Level one, such as the tailor shop, allowed a man to receive 12 cents per hour, while someone at a less-skilled job at level four, such as cell house maintenance, might make 5 cents per hour.

Inmates lived by a strict timetable. The daily routine never varied during the prison's 29-year history. Here is an abbreviated daily prison routine.

6:30 a.m.	Morning gong to get up, get dressed, and straighten cell.
6:50 a.m.	Gong meant that inmates faced cell doors for stand-up count. Cell doors were then opened.
6:55 a.m.	Lined up and marched single file to dining hall.
7:00 a.m.	Breakfast.
7:20 a.m.	Breakfast ended. All silverware was checked by officers. Inmates were marched out of dining hall. Shop working inmates proceeded to rear door that led to the prison yard and shops. Inside workers proceeded to their work stations and stood by. During all the inmates' movements, there were several officers near to see that the procedure went smoothly.
7:25 a.m.	Shop inmates were allowed through the rear cell house door, which led to the prison yard and through a steel door in the yard wall. Inmates then proceeded down a long flight of stairs, through a double full-body metal detector, and on to their assigned shops.
7:30 a.m.	Inmates were counted before work began.
11:30 a.m. to 12:00 noon	Inmates returned to the cell house and marched to the dining hall where they had the noon meal and were then returned to their cells for lock-down and a noon head count.
12:20 p.m.	Inmates proceeded to work details same as in the morning.
4:25 p.m.	All inmates in shops returned to the prison by way of the metal detectors and marched to the dining hall for evening meal.
4:50 p.m.	Inmates marched to cells for final lock-down. A stand-up count was taken.

From that point on, cell head counts continued every half hour, until the next morning when the procedure started all over again. Lights were turned out at 9:30 p.m.

Inmates were expected to shave three times a week. They were allowed to have their own shaving mugs. The blades were furnished by an officer. The inmates had to return the blade in exactly one-half hour or else! Mainline inmates, as officers called inmates who obeyed the rules, were allowed three showers a week, while isolation confinement inmates were allowed only one per week. Food handlers showered daily. Inmates received haircuts once a month.

PRISON YARD OFFERS GAMES, SPORTS

Officers Guard Against Attacks by Inmates

The prison yard was located at the northwest end of the cell house. Different inmates were in the yard at various times. On weekdays most of the inmates who were locked all the time in isolation confinement, D Block, were allowed in the yard to exercise. They were kept in small groups and were closely supervised. When the general inmate population was in the yard, they had a number of activities to choose from such as baseball, chess, or checkers, or they could just sit around.

The most popular game among the prisoners was handball. There were two courts. One was for experienced players and the other for novices. Yard time was considered a privilege by the prison administration. With any disciplinary hearing, an inmate could lose yard time at once. That privilege would then have to be earned all over again.

The prison yard was enclosed by thick concrete walls approximately 15 feet high with a fence extending several feet beyond, topped with barbed wire. There was a "catwalk" which ran the complete length of the yard outside the fence. This catwalk allowed officers from two towers to observe inmates in the yard. Although officers were always present among the inmates in the yard, they were never armed. This was a dangerous place to be whenever violence, such as a stabbing, occurred. Officers never allowed inmates to walk directly to them in the yard, and when they walked around the yard, inmates were to move out of their way. (Refer to page 59.)

Right: Typical cell where inmates spent up to 13 hours a day. B and C Blocks

Right: Isolation confinement cell where inmates were locked up most of the time except for showers and one hour a week in the yard. This cell was 25 percent larger than top cell. D Block

Alcatraz Island: Maximum Security

Above: D Block or the Treatment Unit, as it was officially called. There were 36 isolation cells and six "dark" or "hole" cells (doors closed). Door at the end of the corridor led to the library – 1941.

1. Main Cell House
2. Prison Yard
3. Kitchen
4. Dining Room
5. Six Dark Cells
6. Library
7. Administration
8. Warden's Office
9. West Road Tower
10. West Gun Gallery
11. East Gun Gallery
12. Utility Corridor (where three inmates were killed)
13. Hospital (above kitchen and dining room)
14. Door that leads to Prison Yard from Cell House
15. Armory
16. Two hostage cells, '46 Riot

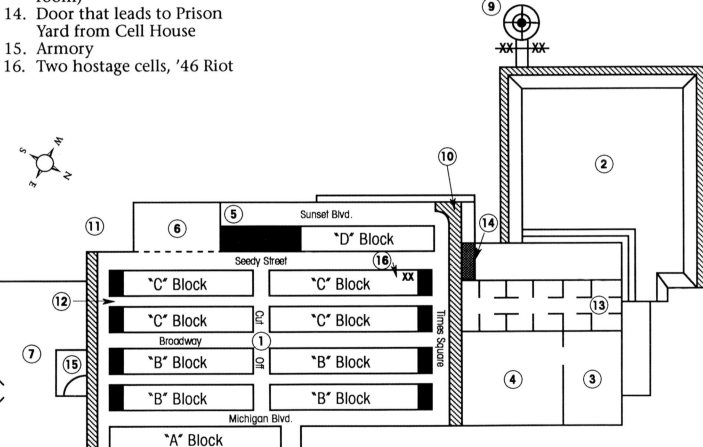

NOT TO SCALE

CELLS CARVE UP PRISON POPULATION
Violators Kept in Isolation

The main area of any prison is the cell house. Alcatraz Island had a total of four cell blocks. (Refer to diagram on preceding page.) There was the old army or A Block. This block was not upgraded when Alcatraz became a federal prison. As one tours the cell house today, one will notice the sharp contrast between the bars in A Block and the bars of the remaining three blocks. The flat bars in A Block were installed in 1910. The block was used on a limited basis by the federal prison. Beginning about 1948, inmates were allowed to use A Block to type such documents as briefs for court or letters to their lawyers. The block was also used by the staff to temporarily house inmates who were going to make court appearances or were about to be transferred.

Both B and C Blocks were three tiers high, and each was divided into two sections, allowing for a cutoff passageway which ran between them. This cutoff permitted the officer to pass from one side of the cell house to the other very quickly. Almost all of the general inmate population were housed in these two cell blocks.

The fourth cell block was D Block or the Treatment Unit as it was sometimes called by prison officers. This block was also three-tiered, but unlike B or C Blocks, it faced only one way — west. D Block was only one section long and contained 36 isolation cells and six solitary or "hole" cells. Men who were confined to any of the 36 isolation cells were segregated from the main prison population and were kept in their cells at all times. The only exception to this was an hour in the yard and a shower once a week. The inmates confined here were fed all three meals in their cells. These cells were about 25 percent larger than the cells in either B or C Blocks.

The size of the D Block cells was the result of a complete reconstruction job in 1939-40 after five men attempted an escape from this section. Inmates in D Block were in isolation for several reasons, such as: violations of prison rules and regulations, confrontations with officers or other inmates, or an escape attempt. How long these men would spend in D Block was determined by prison officials.

Above: Six hole or dark cells solitary confinement

Above: Enclosed west gun gallery at northwest end of D Block

The remaining six cells on the bottom tier of D Block were called "hole" cells. Inmates referred to them mostly as the "hot box." Five of these cells contained fixtures such as toilets and wash basins. However, the inmates began damaging them, so everything was removed. The sixth cell had always been empty except for a drain hole in the center of the floor. This cell was called the "strip cell" and was used when officers were dealing with an incorrigible or violent inmate. All his clothes were removed, and he was placed in a cell. Usually at night he would be given a blanket and mattress. If he continued to cause trouble by stopping up the drain hole, then these, too, were removed.

All six solitary cells had one thing in common: each had two metal doors. The inner door was grated, but the outer one was solid steel, and when it was closed, the inmate could be left in total darkness. The lights in these cells were controlled from the outside, and most of the time they were left on during the daylight hours. Inmates were kept in the "hole cells" up to three weeks, depending on the severity of the rule that was violated.

All the cell blocks ran in a north-south direction with the cells facing either east or west. There were two gun galleries in the cell house. There were the east and west gun galleries, and they both were situated so the officer assigned could observe walkways in front of the cells. The west gun gallery was multileveled, so the officer could observe all three tiers of each cell block. Although officers assigned to the two gun galleries were armed, they were separated from the cell house by bars and wire mesh. Officers were never permitted within the cell house itself with any type of firearm.

Right: B and C Blocks. The aisle between was called "Broadway" by the inmates.

Alcatraz Island: Maximum Security

Right: The cell block cutoff looking from east to west.

Below: C Block showing all three tiers

OFFICERS LIKE PRISONERS' TASTY FOOD

Tear Gas Available for Dessert In Case of Disturbances

The only events that broke up the otherwise dull routine were the three trips inmates made to the dining hall each day. There were few complaints about the food. My father often told me that on many occasions when he was assigned to the kitchen or the dining hall, he would eat a meal. He said the food served to the inmates was the best he had eaten at any other prison in the federal system.

During the thirties and forties inmates went through a serving line and then sat at long tables. Until 1937 the "rule of silence" was in place. Talking was not permitted. By the fifties, inmates were not only talking, but enjoyed a modern cafeteria-style of dining offering wider choices. In the mid-fifties a small combo band would play at meals on special occasions like Christmas. There were four rules all inmates had to adhere to while in the dining room:

1. No loud talking.
2. Whatever food you took, you ate. Wasting food would bring disciplinary measures quickly.
3. Twenty minutes was allowed for meals.
4. All silverware was accounted for before inmates left the dining hall.

Above: Kitchen

Inmates marched to and from the dining hall. Because inmates had only 20 minutes for each meal, they found little time left for anything else. As the dining hall afforded the best location for a disturbance, the short eating period helped to put a damper on this type of activity. The biggest deterrents to disturbances in the dining hall, however, were the tear gas canisters that Warden Johnston had installed on the ceiling beams in the dining hall. They were in plain view of the inmates and could be released automatically by an officer outside the dining hall area. Because of these canisters, inmates referred to the dining room as the "gas chamber."

Right: Dining hall in the '30s and '40s

Left: Dining hall in the '50s. Note the gas canisters, top center.

Alcatraz Island: Maximum Security

BOOKS AND BIBLES ALLOWED IN CELLS
Books To Dream On and Prayers To Hope On

As there was no radio or television in the early days of "The Rock" during the thirties and forties, inmates had very little to occupy their free cell time period from 5:00 p.m. to 9:30 p.m. (lights out). Fortunately, the Army had left a well-stocked library when it turned the island over to the Bureau of Prisons. There were several thousand books to begin with in the library, and by 1960 it had grown to 15,000 books of every description imaginable. Inmates were allowed to have a total of three library books in their cells along with a Bible, dictionary, and other study books. Each inmate was issued a library card. Failure to return books on their due dates usually resulted in loss of one's library privileges. Books, and later magazines, were all ordered from one's cell. Lists were given to each inmate. The materials were all delivered by inmates who worked in the library.

The prison chapel was located on the second floor just above the administration offices. Access to the chapel, however, was not gained by inmates walking through the administration offices, but through a red stairwell at the southwest end of the cell house. Catholic and Protestant services would alternate each week. Starting in the 1940s, movies were shown to the inmates once a month. Later, movies were shown twice a month and on holidays. Care was taken to show only certain movies to the inmates, such as musicals or comedies. During the fifties, as prison regulations relaxed somewhat, inmates were given permission to form a small prison band. They were allowed to practice on weekends in the prison chapel. An inmate group attempted to form a band during the mid-'30s; however, it was short-lived.

Within the prison administration building area was the armory. This bullet-proof enclosure was the prison's communication center. All foot traffic into the main cell house and officer reporting went through the armory.

Above: Prison armory

Left: Prison library

Right: Prison chapel

BOATS SERVE AS KEY LINK TO SAN FRANCISCO

Prisoners Do Laundry for Nearby Army Bases

The dock area was always one of the busiest locations on Alcatraz. However, it reached its peak during World War II when the prison did laundry for the San Francisco Army Presidio, Angel Island, and Fort Mason, as well as the island's employees and their dependents. As inmates were not allowed to handle the off-loading of cargo from ships docked at Alcatraz, several additional officers had to be assigned to the dock at peak shipment times. The ship that brought most of the laundry to the prison during the war was the *General Frank M. Coxe*, an army steamship built during the twenties.

Below: A rare view of the General Frank M. Coxe *docked at Alcatraz in 1940. The dock size later expanded.*

There were several small ships which docked at Alcatraz Island for one reason or another, mostly during the thirties and forties. Because the prison had no source of fresh water, it was transported to the island by water ships called the *El Aquador and* the *El Aquario.* The two ships alternated, each carrying several thousand gallons of water to the island every two weeks. The water was pumped to a 250,000 gallon storage tank that was completed in 1939. After World War II the two water ships were replaced by a multipurpose water barge. This barge, which had an enclosure around its deck, was able not only to carry water and fuel, but also supplies.

There were two prison launches. The *McDowell* had been given to the Bureau of Prisons in 1934 by the U.S. Army when Alcatraz became a federal prison. The second launch was built by McNeil Island Federal Prison labor in 1945 and was named in honor of Alcatraz's first warden, Warden Johnston. This launch was presented to Warden Johnston by McNeil's warden, Paul Squier, the author's uncle. The prison launches were used to transport prison personnel and their dependents to and from Pier 4 in San Francisco at Fort Mason.

As there were no schools on the island, all school-age children had to make the round trip by launch each school day. They left for school on the 7:20 a.m. or 8:10 a.m. boat and returned to the island on the 3:35 p.m. boat.

The prison launches averaged a trip to and from Pier 4 about every hour during the day with the first boat leaving the island at 6:45 a.m. and the last boat leaving Pier 4 at Fort Mason at 12:25 a.m. Missing the last boat meant spending the night in San Francisco. There were only three reasons that would cause the boat schedule to be changed or canceled. The first might occur if several prisoners were going to be transferred. The second, when the weather become either too foggy or rough to make the crossing to the mainland. And finally, the schedule would be canceled if an escape attempt was in progress.

Right: The water tower, built to hold 250,000 gallons, was completed in 1939.

Above: The prison's water barge and prison launch,
Warden Johnston – *1949*

Below: Inmates sort laundry on the dock.

Alcatraz Island: Maximum Security

Left: Dock and waiting room at Pier 4, San Francisco

Below: Dock inmate loading truck

PRISON "TROUBLEMAKERS" TRANSFERRED TO "THE ROCK"

Inmates in Transit Shackled and Chained

One event that all residents of Alcatraz witnessed was the transfer of inmates to and from the island. The transfers usually occurred twice a year.

The method by which the transfers were conducted never varied. Strict security was always given top priority. The number of inmates that were to be transferred within the federal system seldom varied. Almost without exception 20 or 22 were removed from the island under heavy guard. The inmates were chained and shackled with heavy leg and wrist irons. By the mid-fifties irons were replaced with hand and leg cuffs. Exactly one month later, "The Rock" would receive the same amount of inmates that were transferred a month earlier. This system was used in order to maintain a constant prisoner population of about 280.

Who were the inmates that replaced those transferred from Alcatraz? Simple—They were the troublemakers at other federal prisons within the system—the ones who attempted escapes, murdered other inmates, assaulted prison officers, etc.

However, the two categories of inmates who were transferred from Alcatraz were quite different. They were men who were due for outright release or parole within six months. Those who had served three to five years trouble-free on the island and had caused no conduct problems were also transfer candidates.

Not all inmates qualified for the second category. Take the cases of Al Capone, George "Machine Gun" Kelly, or Robert "Birdman of Alcatraz" Stroud. These infamous residents of Alcatraz together spent a total of 39 years confined on "The Rock." Each one was eventually transferred due to health problems. The prisoner who claims the record for the longest incarceration on Alcatraz Island was Alvin "Creepy" Karpis, who spent a total of almost 26 years at this island prison. Details of these and other notorious residents of "The Rock" will be related later in the book.

Opposite page: Inmates leaving Alcatraz when it closed in 1963

Observing the newly arrived inmates getting their first look at "The Rock" always made me wonder. No matter how hardened these men seemed to be, they always appeared to be a little intimidated by this twelve-acre rock in the bay. No doubt they had heard many stories from inmates at other prisons.

The new inmates, after boarding trucks, were transported "up top," where the prison was located. After showers, the issuance of inmate uniforms, and general indoctrination, each inmate received a booklet of rules and regulations. He was expected to conform to these rules without deviation. After an interview with the warden, each inmate was assigned to a one-man cell. This is how his integration into the main-stream prison population began. During the first 30 days he appeared in front of a panel of prison officials who determined his work abilities.

OFFICERS WATCH PRISONERS FROM TALL TOWERS

Private Boats Fired Upon If They Strayed Too Close

At one time there were six watch towers on Alcatraz, four of which were manned on a 24-hour basis during the early years of the prison's operation. Following is a list of the watch towers and their locations. Three were on top of buildings, and three were free-standing towers.

1) The main tower was on the roof of the prison at its northeast corner. It was manned 24 hours a day. The tower was removed in 1951. (Refer to picture on page 49.)

2) The model or west industry tower on the roof of the west industry shop building near the northwest corner of the island. It was manned only during daylight hours. This tower still is in place on the roof; however, the tower and the building it sits on are long past the point of repair. (Refer to picture on page 48.)

3) The power house tower was fixed on a built-up platform at the top of a cement block located adjacent to the island power house. It was close to the northeast end of the island. At first the tower was manned on

days only. However, by the 1940s it was abandoned in favor of a newer and higher dock tower where an officer could observe almost the entire east side of the island.

4) The hill tower was near the north center area of the island about one block northwest of the prison yard. It had two catwalks. One ran from the northwest prison yard wall to the tower, while the second catwalk connected the tower with the west industry building. The catwalk allowed the officer mobility to either view inmates in the yard or assist the officer stationed in the model tower. (Refer to picture on page 48.)

5) The west or road tower was located just west of the southwest end of the prison yard. It was connected to the yard catwalk by a 20-foot catwalk of its own. This tower walkway was separated from the prison yard catwalk by a fence that ran completely around the walkway. It had barbed wire all around the fence, also. A gate in the middle of the walkway was controlled electronically by the tower officer. During the " '46 Riot," officers in both the road and hill towers were wounded by rifle fire from within the prison by an inmate. (Refer to picture on page 48.)

6) The dock tower was positioned at the north end of the dock on the east side of the island. It replaced a smaller tower in 1940. The dock tower is still standing today and can be viewed as one steps off any of the tour boats that visits the island daily. The tower, however, is in a sad state of disrepair, as are almost all of the buildings and structures still standing on the island. This tower was one of the highest free-standing prison watch towers ever built. It rises some 60 feet above the dock. The author recalls the officers in this tower actually fired on private boats that strayed within the 200-yard limit of the island. A tower officer gave one warning with a megaphone. If that was ignored, he fired a shot over the bow. If the craft still failed to stop, several armed officers boarded the prison launch, raced out to meet the boat, and seized it. The craft was held for the Coast Guard until they arrived and impounded it. The craft's occupants were held until questioned by the FBI. The dock tower officer always kept possession of the prison launch keys whenever it was docked at the island. (Refer to page 49.)

All watch tower officers reported to the prison armory via inter-island phone once an hour, and also, of course, when he had something important to report.

All tower officers were armed with .45-caliber automatics and 30.06-caliber rifles. In addition, the officers in the dock, hill, and road towers were also armed with automatic weapons (machine guns).

During the prison's 29-year history, four inmates were shot and killed by officers working in watch towers during escape attempts.

Below: Road tower in foreground and hill tower in lower center. Note the tower on the industry building at lower left.

Alcatraz Island: Maximum Security

Above: Dock tower and main tower on top of prison. Note warden's house and lighthouse at top left.

Bottom: Dock area and dock tower

WARDEN JAMES A. JOHNSTON
Alcatraz Island 1934 – 1948

WARDEN EDWIN SWOPE
Alcatraz Island 1948 – 1955

WARDEN PAUL J. MADIGAN
Alcatraz Island 1955 – 1961

WARDEN OLIN BLACKWELL
Alcatraz Island 1961 – 1963

WARDENS USE INCENTIVES TO CURB VIOLENCE

Prisoners' Good Behavior Rewarded by Work and Pay Opportunities

Warden James A. Johnston arrived at Alcatraz Island while it was still an army prison in 1933. He was given the task of turning the old 1912 army prison into a modern escape-proof maximum security penitentiary.

Warden Johnston was no stranger to prisons and had already served as warden of two penitentiaries in California. In 1912 he was assigned to clean up Folsom Prison. Folsom was constructed mostly during the 1890s and, until Johnston arrived, merely housed men up to four in a cell. It was a violent place with killings about as common as catching a cold. Warden Johnston changed all that with one stroke of the pen. He created a prison farm program, and any inmate who proved he could abide by the rules would be allowed to work on it. Penologists of the day were skeptical if the program would work. Well over 75 years have gone by, and the farm program is still working. Next, Johnston was made warden of San Quentin. This job took a little more doing, but Johnston tackled it head-on. He expanded the shops and put in educational guides along with a little religion. This small, soft-spoken man remained at San Quentin until 1925. Then he left the prison system to put his law degree to work in banking in San Francisco. When Johnston answered the call to become Alcatraz Island's first warden, he knew it would go against his nature to run a prison that had minimum privileges and no rehabilitation. However, he took the job, and, as they say, "the rest is history."

The author's father often said that Warden Johnston was a fair but strict man to both officers and inmates. He was called "old salt water" by the inmates, and they respected him. Warden Johnston left Alcatraz in 1948, just two years after the blood bath of the " '46 Riot."

The second warden of Alcatraz was Edwin Swope, who had a wide range of experience as a warden of both federal and state prisons. During the first few years of Swope's administration, policy remained pretty much as Warden Johnston had left it. Swope began to liberalize the prison's system in the early 1950s by first changing the inmates' uniforms. Instead of tailored coveralls, the standard prison uniform would now be blue denim pants with chambray shirts.

Swope also introduced radio earphones into the cells in the main cell blocks, B and C. However, his most notable change was the appointing of black inmates to the kitchen detail. Black inmate isolation within the cell house was also ended.

Warden Swope retired in early 1955 and later accepted a post as warden of New Mexico's state prison.

The next man to assume the duties of warden was Paul J. Madigan, a soft-spoken, well-educated man who was no stranger to Alcatraz. He had been captain on Alcatraz during the late thirties under Warden Johnston. He was promoted to associate warden and transferred to Terminal Island in Southern California.

Madigan returned to Alcatraz Island in 1949 and served under Warden Swope for nearly three years. He was once again transferred but returned to Alcatraz in 1954. In 1955 Madigan gained the stewardship of "The Rock." Under "Promising Paul," as he was called by officers and inmates alike, a trend towards liberalization took place. The nickname resulted because it seemed that whoever needed or wanted something would always receive a "sounds like a good idea to me" or "we will look into that." However, no one's ideas or requests ever seemed to materialize. All in all, Warden Madigan ruled Alcatraz Island with either a firm or gentle hand as the situation dictated. Madigan was transferred from Alcatraz to McNeil Island Federal Penitentiary in Washington as warden in 1961.

The fourth and final warden was Olin Blackwell. Many thought that with the transfer of Warden Madigan to McNeil Island, it was only a matter of time before the curtain would come down on Alcatraz as a federal prison. Some viewed Warden Blackwell's appointment to the top spot on the island as that of a caretaker. Less than 18 months after Warden Blackwell arrived at Alcatraz, it was closed.

Blackwell received his prison administration training at Lewisburg Federal Penitentiary, where he served as captain and associate warden. Blackwell continued the liberalization of Alcatraz. He relaxed certain rules such as more yard time for inmates and less time in the "hole" for offenses that in earlier times would have carried longer stays. Some mistrust built up between a few officers and

Warden Blackwell. Some officers felt that under any of the three previous wardens, the June 11, 1962 so-called "Escape From Alcatraz," would never have taken place. The author has never completely agreed with that assessment. Warden Blackwell arrived at Alcatraz Island at a period when funding cutbacks were the rule of the times within the federal prison system. Alcatraz already needed millions of dollars to restore the prison and most structures around the island and to upgrade officer training and pay in order to maintain (largely a myth by now) a last-resort threat to inmates at other federal prisons. The "kiss of death" came when Attorney General Robert Kennedy called Alcatraz a "dinosaur of the past" and ordered it shut down. So on March 21,1963, the inmates were removed and the prison was closed.

OFFICERS RECEIVE JUDO AND VARIOUS WEAPONS TRAINING

Surprise Searches of Cells Conducted for Weapons, Drugs

The officers assigned to Alcatraz were not just so many names drawn out of a hat. They were usually older officers who had experience at other federal penitentiaries. During the entire 14 years that Warden Johnston served at Alcatraz Island, he personally put his stamp of approval on every officer transferred to "The Rock."

From the federal prison's beginning in 1934 through 1942, newly arriving officers received various forms of physical and mental training. Physical classes were in areas such as firearms, which included the .45-caliber automatic, .30-caliber rifle, gas billy, and automatic weapons like the machine gun. Officers were expected to qualify with the .45-caliber and .30-caliber rifles. Classes in self-defense and aggressive judo were also a part of the curriculum. Classroom lectures in penology, sociology, and psychology were included on the recently arrived officer's schedule. Just as in police academies, a lot of time was devoted to role playing. As officers were always in close proximity to inmates in areas such as the yard, dining hall, and cell house, they were expected to handle any situation that might arise. It was of utmost importance that the officer(s) involved quickly gain the upper hand or they might find themselves suddenly dealing with a full-scale riot.

The harshest form of punishment an inmate could receive, other than for murder or an attempted escape, would be for an assault on a fellow inmate, or even worse, an assault on one of the officers. Attacking an officer resulted in confinement in one of the six "dark" or "hole" cells. This "dark" cell incarceration usually lasted at least two weeks. At the end of that time, a disciplinary board determined the inmate's fate. In a violent confrontation with an officer, it was not unusual for the inmate to be placed in D Block or the "treatment unit" as the 36 cells were called. This would mean a 24-hour-a-day lockdown. Of course, all of the inmate's privileges would be suspended. Confinement to D Block could last up to 18 months. As a result of attempted escapes, some inmates, such as Whitey Franklin, spent as much as eight years in this type of lockdown. Robert "Birdman" Stroud spent almost six years in one of these cells. This was the way Alcatraz was run. There were no favors and no quarter given. You knew that if you broke the rules, especially those that were considered "major incidents," a very high price would be exacted for your indiscretion. Most inmates learned early on that "The Rock's" officials were not here to run some kind of popularity contest. Officers had to maintain a constant awareness that they were dealing with some of the most potentially explosive men ever incarcerated. The possibility of violence was an ever-present companion of every officer. Two dramatic examples of this violence will be shown in the section which deals with escape attempts later in the book. One involved a 1938 escape attempt and the other is related in the description of the " '46 Riot."

The shakedowns of inmates' cells were conducted without notice. Contraband on Alcatraz was not as prevalent as it was in lighter security prisons; however, it did present a problem. Some of the items found in cells included filed-down spoons and forks, money, and from time to time, small amounts of narcotics. Shakedowns usually were conducted while inmates were eating or working.

The author's father noted in his journal in April 1945:

Entered #4-- in C blk. for a shakedown of inmate -----'s cell. After ten minutes, came up empty. While washing hands at wash basin, noticed water drained very slowly. Requested pipe wrench and removed drain coupling. Found set of bendable heavy tin "knuckles." Inmate ----- was immediately placed in isolation cell #--. Knuckles turned over to watch lieutenant. Report made and forwarded to the deputy warden.

Many theories have been put forth as to how contraband entered the prison, especially narcotics and money. It was obvious that some of the items were molded into weapons right in the prison, such as spoons, forks, and chisels. Many prison officials felt that items like money and narcotics arrived in foodstuffs and other supplies sent to the island. When you think about it, there were not too many possibilities, given the strict visitation rules.

INMATES ADAPT TO PRISON RULES
Visitors Forbidden To Touch Prisoners

Alcatraz Island was designed to house some of the most violent and incorrigible men in the federal prison system. If the correctional officer had a strict set of rules and regulations to follow, then the inmates confined on "The Rock" had a much tougher set to adhere to.

During the first three months after an inmate's transfer to Alcatraz, he could have no visitors. After this period, he would be allowed one visit per month. This visit could be with only a blood relative or the inmate's wife. The visitor had to apply in writing in order to visit an inmate. If the the visit was approved, the warden's office would send a letter to the prospective visitor informing him or her to be on the dock at Pier 4 in San Francisco on a certain date and time with the letter to show the boat officer. Once the visitor had arrived on the island, he or she would be driven to the prison. The visitor would then walk through a second full-body metal detector. The first one was at the dock.

The visit was conducted at one of five visitor stations by talking into phones and looking at each other through five inches of bullet-proof glass. There was never any physical contact between visitor and inmate. The inmate was not allowed to talk about anything concerning the prison or its operation. If he violated this policy, he would immediately be cut off by a monitoring officer, and the visit was terminated. This could also result in the suspension of visitation rights for the inmate. Attorneys' visits were cleared through the deputy warden's office. All inmate mail leaving or arriving at the prison was read, and, if need be, censored by prison officials. The "mainline inmates," those who obeyed the rules, were allowed to write two letters per month. Some inmates could write only one letter per month, depending on whether he was involved in disciplinary action.

Above: Visitation stations

Inmates Devise Ingenious Games

The custom in most prisons was, and still is, to maintain a relaxed atmosphere after the evening meal by allowing cell doors in the cell houses to remain open for and hour or two. This allows inmates to visit nearby cells and talk with other inmates. Although most prison officials feel that the movement of contraband and homosexual activities take place during these so-called "free periods," it does allow for tensions to lower and morale to increase.

This practice never occurred on "The Rock," and the only "free period" an inmate on Alcatraz had was when he was either locked in his one-man cell or under close supervision in the prison yard.

Before radio jacks were installed in cells in the mid-fifties, inmates had only library books to look forward to. The books were all delivered to the inmate's cell as noted earlier in the book. As an inmate's time in his cell was his own from lock-up at 4:50 p.m. until lights out at 9:30 p.m., some of the confined men on Alcatraz learned how to read out of sheer desperation. Those who could not read gave up weekend yard time to receive reading instruction from the island priest or minister.

Inmates did dream up ingenious methods to break the hours of monotony. An inmate in one cell would take his bar of soap and draw a square on the wall, usually where the calendar would hang. He would then divide it into the number of squares that were on a checkerboard and number each one. He then would take pieces of toilet paper, wad them up, and put a very small amount of toothpaste on each square of both sides of the board. He was now ready to play checkers. The man in the next cell would do the same. As officer's rounds were every half-hour (one hour in later years), and a game usually would take about 20 minutes, it was perfect. The inmate would walk to the front of his cell and whisper to his neighbor what number he was moving to. Each inmate had both sets of checkers (toilet paper), so they would know where the other man moved. If the game took longer than 30 minutes, they would merely hang the calendar over the game until the officer had made his rounds. By the mid-forties, inmates were allowed to keep checker or chess boards in their cells, but were allowed to play only with the man in the adjoining cell.

Frustrated Inmates Lash Out at Officers and Other Prisoners

It would be a fair statement to say that most inmates were frustrated as soon as they set foot on "The Rock." Most new inmates felt Alcatraz was the end of the line for them, and, in some cases, they were right. The strict rules and regulations, along with extremely few privileges, had a profound and negative impact on some of these men. Some became anxious, depressed, and a few showed more hostility. This was the very thing that first brought most of them to Alcatraz. Even though every inmate who was transferred to Alcatraz Island heard it was impossible to escape, most likely each inmate thought about it at some time or another.

The officers, although by no means psychologists, were trained to spot most behavior patterns. Frustrations now and then manifested themselves into confrontations with other inmates or even sometimes with an officer. Several inmates over the years were targets of stabbings and "head bashings" which usually took place in the prison yard. In many cases, inmates died as a result of such attacks. When an incident of this nature occurred, the inmate "code of silence" was enforced. No one saw a thing. While the incident would be taking place, unarmed officers rushed to break things up, literally putting their lives on the line.

Left: Unarmed officers in the prison yard with a small group of men from D Block isolation unit

There were only a few plus factors for an inmate who was doing time on "The Rock." Almost all the inmates liked the idea of only one man to a cell. This may seem somewhat trivial to the reader, but most of the men felt that of all the places in the prison, this five-foot by nine-foot cell belonged to him alone. It was his only, even if he had no control over who and when someone would enter it. Just about every inmate on the island looked forward to the three meals each day. The food was always well above the standards set by the Federal Bureau of Prisons. The one other plus factor about doing time on this island of rock was the fact that there were enough jobs around if an inmate wanted to work, and after 1942, he received compensation for working.

Alcatraz Climate Poses Health Hazard to Officers, Inmates Alike

One of the things that all inmates disliked, and said so on many occasions, was the constant cold and dampness of the entire cell house. Most of the time it felt as cold inside the cell house as it did outside in the prison yard. Inmates who were assigned to the ground floor cells of each block, or "the flats" as they were called, would put in transfers to second or third tier cells. The reason for this was a simple one: steam heat in the cell house would rise, and the higher the cell, the warmer it was. Cells on the second- and third-tiers were always quieter because there was less foot traffic. By the time several of the inmates were transferred from Alcatraz Island, they had developed bronchitis, rheumatism, and many other conditions related to a constant damp climate. Inmates were not alone with these conditions. Officers who worked and lived on "The Rock" also made the same complaints, The author recalls his father telling him on many occasions that he had gotten rheumatism from working and living on the island for 11 years. As the author was 18 years old when he moved from Alcatraz, he hopes he may have avoided some of these problems.

Prisoners Establish "Pecking Order"

Every prison in the country, whether state or federal, has its own social scale or structure. In a state prison an inmate serving time for embezzlement or forgery ranks near the top of the social ladder, which usually guarantees the respect of his fellow prisoners. On the other hand, if he is doing time for child abuse or molestation, he is lucky if he reaches the end of his sentence in one piece. The federal prison system is just about the same with one exception. If an inmate had made the FBI's list of the most wanted "Public Enemy" at sometime prior to his capture, then he enjoyed a special status among his fellow prisoners. The more wanted on the FBI list, the more respect he received. There were several of these top achievers on Alcatraz, especially during the thirties and forties, which included George "Machine Gun" Kelly and Alvin "Creepy" Karpis." By 1950 the list's title was called the FBI's "Ten Most Wanted." These and others received a special status among their fellow inmates. To some of the inmates it was like serving time with living legends.

Inmate Peers Shun Al "Scarface" Capone

Surprisingly enough, Capone, who was the most famous person to serve time in any prison, had it rough on "The Rock" and did hard time on this island prison. In Capone's case it had nothing to do with whether he was on the FBI's most wanted list (which he wasn't). Many of the inmates at Alcatraz did not like his "show off" attitude and his willingness to buy anything he wanted from other inmates. He once offered to buy band members their instruments. In spite of having been a mob king-pin and throwing his money around while in Atlanta Federal Prison, Capone seemed to carry very little weight on an isolated 12-acre island in the middle of San Francisco Bay. Capone was involved in several fights while serving time on Alcatraz, and on one occasion was even stabbed. Even though Capone was unpopular, it would seem unlikely that anyone would seriously consider trying to kill him. After all, a few of these inmates at some point in time would return to Atlanta or Leavenworth Federal Prisons to serve more time or even be released. As Capone's connections in those institutions were still intact, it would be nothing short of suicide to take out "Big Al." Most inmates just tried to avoid him.

Robert "Birdman of Alcatraz" Stroud was in isolation his entire time at Alcatraz and was never allowed to mix with the other inmates. He served his first six years in D Block, and his last 11 years were spent in a large cell in the hospital area. Most inmates admired Stroud just for the fact that he had managed to survive more than 50 years in the system, a majority of which were in isolation. In the next chapter we will discuss some of these infamous inmates of "The Rock."

WHO'S WHO IN CRIMINALS ASSEMBLE ON "THE ROCK"

Officers Mingle with the Likes of Al Capone, "Machine Gun" Kelly, and the "Birdman of Alcatraz"

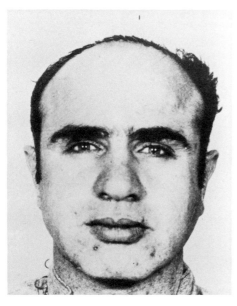

Above: Al "Scarface" Capone

Alfonse "Scarface" Capone AZ#85
Born: 1899
Died: 1947
Time served on Alcatraz Island: Five years
Charge: Income Tax Violations

The author's father got his first glimpse of Capone in the recreation yard at Atlanta Federal Prison in 1933. He had just delivered a prisoner on a transfer to Atlanta from McNeil Island Prison. The watch lieutenant asked my father if he would like to tour the prison before he returned to McNeil. While looking down into the huge recreation yard from a third-floor administration office, my father noticed an inmate with four or five inmates walking near him, but not next to him. When he commented about this, he was told that the inmate was none other than Capone. The lieutenant handed my father a pair of binoculars for a closer look at this most famous of all prisoners. My father later recalled that Capone was a man just under six feet tall with a barrel chest and a stocky build. He must have weighed around 235 pounds. He commented that Capone strutted around the recreation yard as if he were royalty.

Several years later (1939), my father had another occasion to encounter Capone. This time it was on a one-to-one basis. My father had escorted a transferred prisoner to the federal prison at Terminal Island in California and was to return to McNeil Island with a prisoner who was to be transferred from the Terminal Island facility. As court appearances delayed the inmate's departure to McNeil for a period of nearly a month, my father was assigned on a temporary basis to the prison's infirmary. Capone spent a lot of time at the infirmary due to the advanced stages of syphilis taking its toll on his general health. There were two X's on his medical chart by this time which reflected that Capone was in the second of three stages of syphilis.

He was having a rough time of it. He was well aware of what fate held in store for him, but as my father recalled, he talked very little about his disease. He did, however, ramble on about the many good old Chicago days and always felt that people really got only what they wanted during prohibition—"booze." Many of that era would agree.

Sometime later Capone was transferred to the federal prison at Lewisburg where he completed his sentence and was released. He spent some time on the east coast for treatment of his disease, but by this time he was a very sick man. Relatives took him to his estate in Miami, Florida, where he died on January 25, 1947.

Capone first came to the attention of authorities in 1919 when he was only 20 years old. His first brush with the law was for disorderly conduct which was dismissed. Capone rose through the ranks of the mob very quickly until by the late twenties he had most of Chicago's criminal activities under his thumb. For every person who swore that Capone had ordered hundreds of hits (killings), there were even more people who thought of him as some kind of modern day Robin Hood who helped feed and clothe a multitude of widows and orphans. It is a fact that he gave large cash donations to a number of charities.

In 1931 Capone was convicted of U.S. tax violations and was given a 10-year sentence. He began serving his sentence at Atlanta Federal Prison in May 1932. After two years of living almost as well in prison as he did when he controlled his Chicago mob, it was decided by officials at the Bureau of Prisons to transfer Capone out of the public limelight. As the new ultramaximum-security federal prison at Alcatraz Island had just opened in the summer of 1934, some felt that here would be a perfect location to reduce the high visibility Capone had enjoyed at Atlanta. So Capone, along with some other 50 prisoners, was put on a special train to this new escape-proof prison in San Francisco Bay. (Refer to page 23).

As stated in the last chapter, Capone did hard time on "The Rock." During 1938, Capone's health problems became more apparent with symptons of paresis (motor paralysis) caused by syphilis. A spinal tap confirmed doctors' suspicions of Capone's condition.

Capone was transferred to Terminal Island even though he still had more than a year to serve. This was done in order to remove him from the harsh weather on Alcatraz Island and allow him to work on a light-duty status.

It seems almost unbelievable that more than 40 years after Capone's death, movies and television specials are still being produced about this most famous of all American criminals.

*Left: Capone enroute to Atlanta
Prison after his conviction*

*Right: Al Capone's FBI
criminal "rap" sheet*

Alcatraz Island: Maximum Security

George "Machine Gun" Kelly AZ#117
Born: 1895
Died: 1954
Time served on Alcatraz Island: Seventeen years.
Charge: Kidnapping

Another man who served time on Alcatraz Island, and like Al Capone is a legendary criminal figure although for different reasons, was George "Machine Gun" Kelly. As stated earlier, Capone did "hard time" on Alcatraz, while Kelly had it fairly easy, if anyone really had it easy on "The Rock." During his entire 17 years on Alcatraz, Kelly enjoyed the prestige of having been number one on the FBI's "Public Enemy" list. In the federal prison inmate society, that fact alone would bring respect and admiration from most of a prisoner's fellow inmates.

George "Machine Gun" Kelly

My father first met Kelly during the summer of 1942. Kelly had already served eight years on the island, having arrived less than three weeks after Capone. Kelly was described as a man about 5'10" with a round face and a tendency to be a little on the heavy side. He never spoke in a loud or boisterous manner and seemed above average in intelligence. My father told me several years after he had retired that while he (my father) was working on Alcatraz, Kelly had caused no trouble and was a model prisoner.

Kelly suffered a mild heart attack in 1951, so it was decided by prison officials that he should be transferred to Leavenworth Federal Prison. There he could receive better medical treatment. In 1954 Kelly suffered a fatal heart attack. He was within months of being paroled.

The author can recall as though it were yesterday when in 1951 a late afternoon boat was scheduled from Alcatraz Island to Pier 4 in San Francisco. How vividly I can remember a man in leg and wrist irons disembarking from the prison launch while several people pressed closer to get a better look. No one could get any closer than 10 feet of this heavily-guarded and shackled man in a somewhat baggy blue suit. Just before he was helped into the U.S. Marshal's van, he looked right at me and smiled.

One of the off-duty officers who had been waiting on the dock to catch the launch back to the island remarked, "Well, there goes one of our star boarders, "Machine Gun" Kelly." I have never forgotten that sad and gentle smile Kelly gave one very wide-eyed boy.

Kelly was really a small-time crook in Oklahoma, bootlegging whiskey during the 1920s. In 1927 George Barnes, who had adopted his mother's maiden name of Kelly by this time, met his future wife, Kathryn Shannon. Within five years they were married, and to say that she began to dominate his life would be a gross understatement. Kathryn wanted Kelly to rise above his small-time criminal activities and become the most wanted and feared man in the country. Kathryn obtained a Thompson machine gun. She then encouraged Kelly to commit several holdups, which extended throughout several southern states. The one common thing about all the holdups was that Kelly would always display his machine gun during the robberies by waving it around, letting everyone get a chance to see him with it. The newspapers had a field day with that. Kathryn also had his picture taken with the machine gun on numerous occasions. Kelly would sign the back of the pictures, and Kathryn would pass them out to people and, on a least two occasions, sent photos to large newspapers. Kelly told the author's father that Kathryn even wanted to send J. Edgar Hoover one of these pictures.

It did not take long for the legend to take hold. The legend was also helped along by FBI Director J. Edgar Hoover. Hoover, during this era of the Great Depression, had to justify more money and agents in order to fight the criminal element. He seized upon the publicity Kelly was getting and made a little of his own. Every chance Hoover got, he would tell the press this "machine gun-wielding bandit" must be captured. Shortly thereafter, Kelly became the most wanted criminal, crossing state lines to pull his robberies.

Kelly's demise finally came with the kidnapping of Oklahoma oil magnate Charles Urschel in July 1933. His partner was Albert Bates, a long-time robber and burglar. The two entered Urschel's home and found him and his wife playing cards with neighbors. The kidnapers took only Mr. Urschel. He was bound and blindfolded and driven to Kelly's father-in-law's ranch in Texas. Mr. Urschel wrote a ransom note in which Kelly and Bates demanded $200,000 for the safe return of the victim. A short time later the ransom was paid, and Mr. Urschel was released unharmed. Rumor has it that Kathryn wanted to "get rid" of Urschel so he would not identify them. However, Kelly stated that he could recall no talk of ever killing Urschel. It did not take long for Urschel and the FBI to trace Kelly and Bates to Kathryn's father's ranch. Nevertheless, the trio had left sometime earlier. Captured at the scene, though, was Harvey Bailey, who was wanted in connection with the now-famous Kansas City Massacre. Within two months Kelly and his wife were captured in Memphis. Bates was captured in Denver. Kelly, Bates, and Bailey received life sentences, and after a few months in Leavenworth Federal Prison, all three were transferred to Alcatraz Island. Kathryn also received a life sentence and was sent to the women's federal prison at Alderson, W. Virginia.

Some years ago my uncle, Paul Squier, who was warden at McNeil Island Federal Prison for several years, paid my father and mother a visit at their retirement home in Southern California. When my wife and I arrived for dinner, my father and uncle were talking about Kelly. My father was telling about a time when he was assigned to the prison chapel for the Catholic services. Kelly had just finished his duties as an altar boy. Kelly and another inmate were standing at the front of the chapel talking to the priest. The priest was talking to Kelly and said, "George, I know you have been asked this a thousand times. Did you really say to the FBI agents that captured you, 'Don't shoot, G-man, I give up'?" Kelly turned and looked at my father, who was grinning from ear to ear. Kelly then looked at the priest and said, "See, Father, even Mr. Hurley thinks that story is 'crap.'" My father, Kelly, and the other inmate walked out of the chapel, leaving the priest to contemplate the conversation that had just taken place.

Above: George Kelly leaving court after his arraignment on kidnapping charges

Right: George and his wife, Kathryn, being sentenced

Alcatraz Island: Maximum Security

Robert "Birdman of Alcatraz" Stroud AZ#594
Born: 1890
Died: 1963
Time served on Alcatraz Island: Seventeen Years
Charges: Murder

Robert "Birdman of Alcatraz" Stroud arrived on Alcatraz Island in December 1942, just three months after the author's family had moved to the island. Stroud was immediately placed in D Block or the "Treatment Unit" as it was more frequently called by prison personnel. Here, too, as it was at Leavenworth, "The Birdman" was housed in isolation (Cell #42). He would remain in this cell his first six years on "The Rock" (Refer to page 31). He was fed in his cell and allowed one shower a week as were all men locked in isolation. He was allowed a very limited amount of time in the prison yard each week, usually by himself. Only a few inmates who were in isolation were permitted in the yard at any one time. Whenever Stroud was around anyone, which was seldom, he was watched very closely, as prison officials were very aware of his overt homosexual tendencies.

Robert Stroud, "Birdman of Alcatraz"

My father's impression of Stroud during Stroud's early years on the island was that Stroud held most everything in the prison system with contempt. He encouraged other inmates within earshot to cause any type of disruption to the orderly routine that was on Alcatraz. Most of Stroud's actions were the result of Warden Johnston's refusal to allow him to have or care for any birds or other animal in his cell.

Stroud read everything he could get his hands on. Mostly, however, he was interested in books which dealt with the law. Although Stroud had a very limited formal education, he had a rated intelligence quotient over 130. The author's father knew him from 1942 until retiring in 1953. His notes on Stroud in part reflected Stroud's intelligence:

> Had he not been in segregation all these years, he (Stroud) would have been a very successful jail-house lawyer.

The "Birdman's" health began to deteriorate from too many years confinement to the damp environment of D Block. He had for some time been suffering from kidney problems and occasional gall bladder attacks. In 1948 Stroud was removed from his cell in the treatment unit and placed in a hospital cell which was considerably larger and drier.

During a 15-month period between 1951 and 1952, Stroud attempted suicide twice. Once he over-medicated himself with gall bladder medicine he had accumulated instead of taking, and on a second occasion, cut an artery inside his thigh.

Below: Robert Stroud just after leaving Alcatraz Island enroute to Springfield medical facility, 1959

Alcatraz Island: Maximum Security

Stroud's health continued on a downward spiral until 1959 when it was decided by prison officials to transfer him to the medical facility at Springfield, Missouri. Bird lovers had not forgotten Stroud while he was on "The Rock," so when he was transferred, they again began to clamor for his unconditional release from prison. Pressure was put on the Federal Bureau of Prisons and even the U.S. Congress itself. A movie of his life called The Birdman of Alcatraz was released in 1962 to further publicize his 50 years of incarceration, most of which were spent in isolation. The publicity was of no avail, however, as Stroud died quietly in the prison hospital on November 21, 1963. It has been reported that Stroud's last words were, "I do not fear death, as it is the only way I will ever be free."

Stroud was born in Seattle. His early life as a boy was very hard. His family was poor, and he was never able to get along with his father. By the time he was 17 years old, he had run away from home three times. After turning 18 in 1908, he joined a construction company headed for Alaska. When the job ended the same year, Stroud, who was living in the town of Cordova, had come down with pneumonia. He was befriended by a dance hall girl named Kitty, who nursed him back to health. The two of them moved to Juneau where Kitty took a job at a dance hall.

In 1909 Kitty was raped and severely beaten by a bartender named Von Dahmer. Stroud became enraged, got hold of a gun, and went to the hall in order to threaten Von Dahmer. A struggle ensued, and Von Dahmer was shot to death. Stroud pled guilty to manslaughter and received a 12-year sentence. As Alaska was a federal territory in 1909, Stroud was sent to the federal prison at McNeil Island at age 19 to serve his sentence. While at McNeil, Stroud stabbed another inmate during a fight. The other inmate was not hurt seriously; however, another six months was tacked onto Stroud's sentence. He was transferred to Leavenworth Federal Prison in 1912. He had been at Leavenworth only a short time when he was discovered making crude knives for other inmates. He also made an unsuccessful escape attempt.

In 1916 a relative of Stroud's traveled from the west coast to visit him. However, because Stroud had lost his visiting rights due to violation of rules, he was not allowed to receive the visit. The next day in the mess hall during the noon meal, Stroud stood up and walked over to the officer who had earlier put him on report and repeatedly stabbed the officer with a prison-made knife in front of nearly

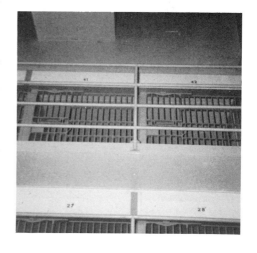

Above: "Birdman's" cell in D Block isolation 42 from 1942 – 1948 (top right)

2,000 witnesses. The officer died later of multiple wounds. Stroud was charged with first degree murder. There were three trials in federal court. The first two trials resulted in convictions, yet both were set aside. The third trial also ended in a conviction, and Stroud received the death penalty. He was sentenced to hang in November of 1919.

Mrs. Stroud's plans for her son did not include death by hanging or any other unnatural death. After several attempts to see the President's wife, Mrs. Woodrow Wilson, she was finally granted an audience with the First Lady. She pled her case as one mother to another. It must have worked because a short time later, President Wilson commuted Stroud's sentence from death to life imprisonment. Because of his hostile and sometimes violent nature, Stroud was to be kept away from other inmates and officers alike as much as possible. Stroud's sentence was interpreted by officials to mean that he was to spend the rest of his life in solitary confinement.

Robert Stroud began his isolation sentence at Leavenworth Penitentiary in a cell 6-feet wide by just over 11-feet long. Prison officials allowed him to draw "get well" and "happy birthday" cards which his mother was permitted to sell on his behalf. One day while Stroud was in the prison exercise yard, he came across two young sparrows flapping their wings in an attempt to fly. As Stroud could not find a nest, he returned with the two young birds to his cell. He managed to keep the two sparrows alive, thus launching his prison career to the care and breeding of small species of birds. Birds began to occupy all his waking moments. He received permission from the warden to breed birds so that he could study diseases that affected different species. Eventually Stroud's bird operation covered the entire space of two prison cells. He finally decided to put all his notes together and publish a book. The book, *Digest of the Diseases of Birds,* can still be found in print in pet stores and libraries throughout the country. Stroud enjoyed corresponding with bird lovers and became a recognized expert in the field.

The Federal Bureau of Prisons decided to shut down Stroud's bird operation because other prisoners also wanted different types of pets in their cells. Stroud told a visitor friend, Della Jones, of the prison's intentions. She, along with bird lovers everywhere, raised so much commotion that prison officials backed down.

Stroud's mother and his brother felt that the Jones woman was trying to dominate Stroud, so they both packed up and headed for the family home in Illinois. To this writer's knowledge, Stroud never saw his mother again.

Stroud became more hostile with prison officials after his mother moved away. He began to violate prison rules and regulations on a regular basis. Officials viewed the violations as a good opportunity to again shut down Stroud's bird operation and transferred him to the ultramaximum facility at Alcatraz Island. As stated earlier, he was transferred to "The Rock" in December 1942.

It is ironic that Stroud will always be remembered as "The Birdman of Alcatraz" even though to the author's knowledge Stroud never so much as held a bird, dead or alive, for the entire 17 years he spent on Alcatraz Island.

Alvin "Creepy" Karpis AZ#325
Born: 1908
Died: 1979
Time served on Alcatraz Island: Twenty-six years
Charge: Kidnapping

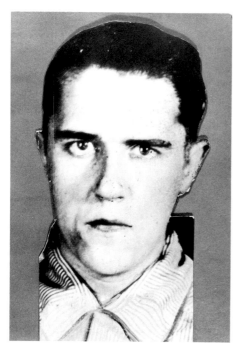

Alvin "Creepy" Karpis

Alvin "Creepy" Karpis, who was convicted of kidnapping and bank robbery, was sent to Alcatraz in August 1936. Fred Hunter AZ#402 was part of the Karpis gang and was with him when he was captured in New Orleans on May 1, 1936. He soon followed Karpis to Alcatraz. In 1943 Hunter, along with four others, attempted an escape. During the attempt, one was killed and one was wounded. All were returned to the island.

As stated earlier, Karpis, along with the likes of "Machine Gun" Kelly, Floyd Hamilton AZ#523 (bank robbery), and several others, enjoyed status on Alcatraz because of their prior "Most Wanted" standing by the FBI. Unfortunately for Karpis, he did an excessive amount of bragging his first few years on "The Rock," which in turn resulted in several fights with other inmates. He began to calm down, and for the last 20 of his 26 years at Alcatraz, he enjoyed his status in the prison society. Be assured, this status enjoyed by certain inmates only extended to other inmates. To prison officials and officers they were just numbers and treated no differently from any other inmate.

When Karpis first arrived on Alcatraz, he was greeted by the only surviving son of "Ma" Barker of the famous Barker gang. He was the youngest Barker son, called "Doc," who was already in custody when "Ma" Barker and her eldest son were killed in a shoot-out with the FBI in a Florida swamp.

Karpis had earlier been a part of the Barker gang, so he and "Doc" knew each other well. Barker was killed in an attempted escape from Alcatraz in 1939. Barker had wanted Karpis to participate in the escape, but Karpis had declined after watching a 1937 attempt by two inmates named Cole and Roe enter the water from an industry building and slip under the surface never to be seen again. Karpis always maintained that to attempt an escape by way of the cold water and swift moving current of San Francisco Bay would be nothing short of suicide.

I once asked my father how Karpis received his nickname "Creepy." I remember my father laughing over this. He recalled that once in the prison yard another inmate called him "Creepy," and Karpis slugged him in the mouth. Everyone knew that Karpis hated the nickname. My father told me that he had heard several different stories as to how he had gotten the name, but he was inclined to believe the one told to him by Hunter, who was with Karpis when he was captured.

Hunter was in isolation D Block after a foiled April 1943 escape attempt in which he had been involved. My father, who was working the Treatment Unit D Block during the summer of 1943, had just been let out of Rufus "Whitey" Franklin's #9 "hole" cell along with another officer. It seems that during the supper meal (served in cells to men in isolation) he had choked on a piece of meat that had gone down the wrong way. Franklin had been in isolation over five years because of a foiled escape attempt in May 1938 in which Franklin had killed an officer, Royal Cline, by hitting him in the head with a hammer. As my father began one of the many swing or evening shift counts of the inmates who were located on the three tiers of D Block, 36 cells in all plus the six hole cell,* he was motioned to wait a minute in front of Hunter's cell. Hunter asked my father how long my father thought he would remain in isolation. My father told him that he would be there until prison officials felt that he was ready to be returned to the main prison population. My father told me that as he started to move along the tier, he stopped and returned to Hunter's cell. My father recalls saying, "Hunter, answer a question will you?' Hunter replied, "If I can, Mr. Hurley." He then asked Hunter how Karpis had received his nickname of "Creepy." Hunter told my father that he thought Karpis had gotten his nickname from "Ma" Barker's oldest son, Freddy, with whom he had done time in Kansas. He advised my father the next time he was around Karpis to look at his eyes and watch them stare right through you. My father had a chance to take Hunter up on his suggestion.

---

*Seldom were the 36 isolation or 6 hole cells ever full. Whitey Franklin served eight years in solitary confinement, over six of which were in "dark" cell #9 with the front metal door left open after D Block had been remodeled in 1940.

A few months later he was transferred to the kitchen where Karpis was also assigned. My father grinned at me and told me that Karpis did have a pair of the beadiest eyes he had ever seen.

Karpis was on the wrong side of the law from the time he could distinguish good from evil. He was in and out of reform schools most of his adolescent life. He made it a practice to escape from every one of them. As he reached adulthood, he graduated from petty crimes to burglary, bank robbery, kidnapping, and even murder. Many law enforcement officers have believed that Karpis was responsible for the Kansas City Massacre, which occurred at the train depot. Federal agents were escorting one Frank Nash, a violent criminal, through the depot in the early thirties when gunfire erupted near the train platform. When the gunfire ended, Nash, along with three agents, was left dead. It was never possible to link Karpis with the crime.

As mentioned earlier, Karpis met Barker in the Kansas State Penitentiary during 1930. Karpis was released in 1931, and the crime wave began. Karpis joined the Barker gang, which included Freddy and his younger brother, "Doc" Barker.

After a few bank robberies, the gang decided to kidnap Paul W. Hamm, President of the Hamm's Brewing Company in St. Paul. The kidnapping took place and a ransom of $100,000 was paid.

In 1934 the gang pulled off another kidnapping for ransom by taking Ed Bremer, who was a bank president, also in St. Paul. The ransom was paid, and this time the gang netted $200,000; however, the FBI had marked the bills. Other robberies by the gang resulted in the deaths of at least five people, including two police officers. The gang split up in late 1934 after hearing that a special task force of federal agents, headed by Melvin Purvis was on the gang's trail.

"Doc" Barker was captured by Purvis in Chicago on January 8, 1935. He was convicted of the Bremer kidnapping and sentenced to life imprisonment at Alcatraz Island. He was later killed in a 1939 escape attempt. His brother Freddy returned to his mother's hideout only to be killed by the FBI along with her in a violent shootout.

It took nearly 18 months longer to catch Karpis, who was by now, the "Most Wanted" on the FBI's list. As noted earlier, he was captured along with Hunter in a parked auto on the streets of New Orleans on May 1, 1936.

During the capture, FBI Director J. Edgar Hoover told the press that he personally handcuffed Karpis. Karpis always disputed this. He stated that none of the agents even had handcuffs and had to use their ties to secure Hunter and himself.

After a speedy trial, Karpis was convicted of kidnapping and sent directly to Alcatraz Island. He spent a total of 26 years on "The Rock," which was longer than any other inmate in the island's 29-year history. He was transferred to McNeil Federal Penitentiary in 1962 and was released in 1969. He was immediately deported to his country of birth, Canada. He wrote two books about prisons, especially Alcatraz. One of the books was a bestseller, which allowed him to move to Spain sometime around 1972. It has been rumored that he died by his own hand in 1979.

Right: FBI mug shots of Alvin "Creepy" Karpis

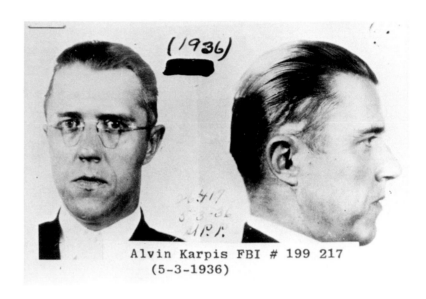

Alvin Karpis FBI # 199 217
(5-3-1936)

Left: FBI capture of Karpis in the streets of New Orleans, May 1, 1936

"Bonnie and Clyde" Survivor Joins Alcatraz Fraternity

Above: Floyd Hamilton

Floyd Hamilton AZ#523 was a bank robber serving 30 years. He hit the magic #1 on the FBI's list while a member of the Bonnie Parker and Clyde Barrow gang. Floyd and his brother, Ray, grew up with Bonnie and Clyde in Texas around the Dallas area. Of the four, Floyd was the only one to survive. As most everyone knows, Bonnie and Clyde were ambushed by a posse of federal and sheriff's officers. They both died in a hail of bullets as they drove up a country road. Floyd's brother lasted for a little longer, but then was convicted of murder and ended up in the Texas electric chair. Only Hamilton survived. Even if he was doing time on "The Rock," at least he was alive.

My father's journal reflects that Hamilton was tall, thin, and a quiet type who spoke with a drawl. Certainly not the type he expected would hook up with the likes of Bonnie Parker and Clyde Barrow.

While on Alcatraz, Hamilton participated in the ill-fated escape attempt in April 1943. Hunter, Karpis's crime partner, was also involved. All 14 escape attempts from Alcatraz will be covered in the next chapter.

Hamilton survived his long stay with the federal prison system and was released in 1958. He returned to the Dallas area where he lived more than 25 years as a free man. He died in the mid-eighties.

Last of the Train Robbers Does Short Stretch

Below: Roy Gardner

Roy Gardner AZ#110 was just about the last of the old-time train robbers. His career of crime dated back to the turn of the century. He was caught committing a burglary and given a two-year sentence in the reformatory. Here began his uncanny ability to escape confinement. After twice escaping the reformatory, he decided to return and serve his time. Later he deserted the U.S. Army and began running guns for outlaws during the Mexican Revolution. He was captured by the Mexican army, but while enroute to the firing squad, he managed to escape and return to the U.S.

In 1920 he was arrested for robbing a mail messenger in San Diego. Gardner was caught trying to bury the mail bag. He was tried and given 25 years at McNeil Island

Federal Penitentiary. While enroute by train in the company of two marshals, Gardner grabbed one of the officers' guns and forced them to undo his leg and wrist irons. Gardner then cuffed the two marshals to a railing. He left the train at Portland. One year later Gardner held up a Roseville postal clerk for $75,000. Several days later he repeated the robbery and netted himself almost $200,000. He was caught a few days later and again given 25 years in prison also to be served at McNeil Island. He was escorted this time by two deputies. Just outside Portland, Gardner pulled a small hand gun from his ankle, and he made a second almost identical clean getaway from the same location. However, Gardner's escape was short-lived. He was recaptured a few days later and this time finally made it to McNeil. He told authorities that he would not be at the prison long.

After only a couple of months at McNeil, Gardner and two other inmates were watching a Labor Day prisoner baseball game, when all of a sudden the three made a dash for the prison's perimeter fence, about 100 yards away. During this daring daylight escape, one inmate was shot and killed, while a second was shot in the leg and unable to make it to the fence. Gardner, however, climbed over the fence, made it to the bay, and swam to freedom.

Just over two months later, Gardner attempted to hold up a U.S. Mail car near Phoenix. The mail clerk overpowered Gardner, took his gun, and held him for police. Gardner pled guilty and was sentenced to Leavenworth Penitentiary for a period of 25 years to run concurrently with his two previous sentences. After four years of literally causing hell at Leavenworth, Gardner was transferred to Atlanta Federal Prison in 1925. In 1928 Gardner and three other inmates attempted an escape by trying to scale the prison wall. Having failed, Gardner was transferred back to Leavenworth and finally settled down. The Bureau of Prisons, though, had had enough of Gardner. In 1934 he was sent to the new federal prison at Alcatraz Island, arriving with the same group that brought Kelly to "The Rock." Gardner worked hard at Alcatraz and had one of the shortest stays in the island's history, two years. He was returned to Leavenworth in 1936 and paroled in 1938. He returned to the Northern California area where he worked on a farm for awhile. Then during the San Francisco World Exposition of 1939 he opened a booth called "Crime Does Not Pay." It was a flop.

On January 10, 1940 Gardner checked into a San

Francisco hotel and checked out of this life by dropping cyanide tablets into water. He left a note stating that he was tired of the struggle. When his body was found, Gardner had just over $3 on his person.

BOLD PRISONERS BOLT FOR FREEDOM

Inmates Brave Frigid Water and Officers' Bullets in Escape Attempts

FOURTEEN MAJOR ATTEMPTS INVOLVING 36 MEN*

Even though "The Rock" was publicized as an escape-proof prison, it neither stopped inmates from talking about or, in a few cases, attempting it.

There probably would have been more than the 14 escape attempts, but for two reasons. First, there was the average cold temperature of the waters in the San Francisco Bay of 53°F. Secondly, the current in and out of the Golden Gate could run as fast as nine miles per hour, sometimes accompanied by deadly undertows. Most prison officials felt that because of these two facts, the waters of San Francisco Bay provided a deterrent equal to an extra 10 invisible correctional officers.

RESULTS OF THE FOURTEEN ESCAPE ATTEMPTS

Shot and killed..7
Shot and wounded................................2
Confirmed drowned.............................1
Presumed drowned 5
Executed in gas chamber 2
Recaptured injured not by gunfire 2
Recaptured not injured.........................17

Right: Sign at south end of island warning anyone who assists an inmate to escape

*Two of the men involved in a 1941 escape attempt, Joseph Cretzer and Sam Shockley, were also involved in the "Riot of '46."

ATTEMPT #1
April 27, 1936
Joseph Bowers AZ#210

Above: Joseph Bowers

Joseph Bowers is credited with the first escape attempt from "The Rock." He was a quiet man and always kept to himself. It was generally believed by most other inmates that Bowers was insane and should never have been sent to Alcatraz. He was a powerful man; however, he seemed to be far below average in I.Q. .

Bowers had been sentenced to 25 years for robbing a grocery store/post office, which made the crime a federal offense. Luck was bad all the way for Bowers that day as the holdup had netted less than $20.

After being sent to Alcatraz, Bowers was assigned to burning trash at the incinerator located on the west side of the island. The incinerator was surrounded by a 12-foot-high cyclone fence topped with barbed wire. The incinerator was within view of the officer in the road tower.

Just before 11 a.m. on April 27, 1936, the road tower officer, Chandler, was surprised to see Bowers climbing to the top of the cyclone fence. The officer shouted several times for Bowers to stop climbing; however, his shouting was in vain. Bowers climbed over the top of the fence and started down the other side. The officer fired a couple of warning shots over Bowers' head. As this failed to halt him, Chandler fired at his legs. Unfortunately, the shot went high, catching Bowers in the right side of his chest causing him to lose his grip on the fence. Bowers fell to his death on the rocks more than 50 feet below.

This first escape attempt from "The Rock" was just a preview of the 13 that were to follow. These escape attempts would result in the violent deaths of many officers and inmates alike over the next 27 years.

ATTEMPT #2
December 16, 1937
Ralph Roe AZ#260
Theodore Cole AZ#258

Ralph Roe, 37, was serving 99 years for bank robbery and other various offenses. He teamed up with an old friend, Theodore Cole, to attempt the second try at escaping from "The Rock." Cole, 26, had been working on a 50 year sentence for kidnapping and several prior escape attempts. Both inmates had been friends at Leavenworth Prison and after several unsuccessful escape attempts, were both transferred to Alcatraz in 1935.

During the early afternoon hours of December 16, 1937, the two inmates, who were assigned to the mat shop, cut their way through a wire mesh window located near the north tip of the island. They squeezed through the opening and dropped to the ground. With a large pipe wrench, they unfastened a gate which was a part of the security perimeter fence. After its removal, the men used the gate by laying it across the sharp rock which allowed them to make their way to the water's edge. The two men slipped into the water of San Francisco Bay during a pea-soup fog with the current running at nearly nine miles per hour. Neither man has ever been seen since. A massive search was conducted for the two inmates.

This escape attempt was witnessed by several other inmates from windows on the north side of the industry building. It was generally believed by most prison officials and inmates who were on Alcatraz at the time, that neither man survived the cold water or fast-moving outbound current. One of the witnesses to the attempt that day was Karpis, who was reported as later commenting, "If I ever try to escape from this rock, it sure won't be by trying to swim the bay." Karpis never did try. He spent 26 years on "The Rock."

There has never been a trace of Roe or Cole; both are officially listed by the Bureau of Prisons to this day as "missing."

Above: Ralph Roe

Below: Theodore Cole

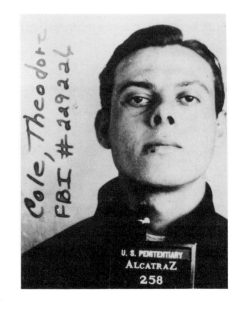

Right: Industry building, northwest end of island

ATTEMPT #3
April 23, 1938
Thomas Limmerick AZ#263
James "Tex" Lucas AZ#224
Rufus "Whitey" Franklin AZ#335

Above: Thomas Limmerick

Below: James Lucas

The third attempted escape from "The Rock" was characterized by a violent act that all too clearly reminded prison officials of the type of hard-core prisoners incarcerated on this island.

Rufus Franklin and James Lucas were both serving 30-year sentences for bank robbery, while Thomas Limmerick was doing life for kidnapping and bank robbery.

About two in the afternoon the three men, who were assigned to the furniture shop, armed themselves with pieces of metal and a hammer. When Officer Royal C. Cline, who was assigned to that area, entered the room, he was jumped and struck on the head with the hammer, crushing his skull. The three inmates then broke out a shop window and climbed to the roof of the building. They encountered some barbed wire which sealed off a catwalk that ran around the roof of the building.

One tower sits flush on top of the industry building's roof. On this day it was manned by Officer Harold Stites, who was later killed in the prison riot of 1946. The three would-be escapees cut the barbed wire and climbed onto the catwalk which led to the industry tower. They began to creep along the catwalk to a point where it ran around the tower. They split up and began attacking the tower with the hammer and pieces of metal just as Officer Stites saw them. Much to their dismay, they realized that the tower glass was shatterproof. Officer Stites, having knowledge that the glass was shatterproof but not bulletproof, pulled his .45-caliber automatic and fired through the glass, striking Limmerick in the head. Franklin again attacked the glass with the hammer. Stites fired again, this time striking Franklin in the arm. As Stites' .45-caliber gun was now empty, he unslung his rifle and fired at Franklin just as he threw the hammer at the tower in a last attempt to break the window, which by now was starting to splinter. Stites fired the rifle, striking Franklin a second time. This ended the assault as inmate Lucas hid next to the tower catwalk when Stites began firing. Other officers arrived and took charge of the scene. Officer Cline and inmates Limmerick and Franklin were taken to the prison hospital.

Officer Cline and inmate Limmerick both died of their

wounds the next day. Franklin recovered from his injuries, and together with Lucas, was tried on murder charges. Each was given a life sentence.

Above: Rufus Franklin

Below: James "Tex" Lucas and Rufus "Whitey" Franklin in court during murder trial, November 1938

Left: Industry tower attacked by Limmerick, Lucas, and Franklin.

ATTEMPT #4
January 13, 1939
Arthur "Doc" Barker AZ#268
Rufus McCain AZ#267
William Martin AZ#310
Dale Stamphill AZ#435
Henri Young AZ#244

Below: Arthur "Doc" Barker

Below: Rufus McCain

Below: William Martin

The leader of the fourth escape attempt from Alcatraz Island was Arthur "Doc" Barker, who was the youngest and only son left of the famous "Ma Barker Gang." Doc's mother and his older brother had been gunned down in a shootout with the FBI sometime earlier.

Barker was serving a life sentence for kidnapping as was Dale Stamphill. William Martin and Henri Young were serving 20 years each for post office robbery, while Rufus McCain was on a 90-year stretch for several bank robberies.

In 1937, under the leadership of Barker, all five inmates were involved in a work strike to improve prison conditions. All five ended up in D Block isolation cells for their trouble. It should be noted that when Alcatraz was converted from an army prison to a federal prison, D Block had not been upgraded with "tool-proof" bars as had B and C Blocks.

On the evening of January 13, 1939, after months of working on the non-tool-proof bars with cutting tools secretly crafted in the prison, all five inmates managed to get out of their cells. With a bar spreader also crafted on the sly, they widened some window bars, broke the window and escaped from the cell house. As the island was shrouded in fog that evening, the inmates had to move slowly in their trek toward the beach on the west side of the island.

The escapees had no sooner arrived at the beach when the prison escape siren began its ear-piercing wail. Within minutes all five were spotted on the beach attempting to tie their clothes to pieces of wood in order to make some sort of raft. By this time the prison launch had been positioned just off the beach with its floodlights turned directly on the shoreline. There were also several armed officers on the cliffs just above where the inmates were located. When officers gave the order to halt what they were doing and give up, Barker and Stamphill made for the water.

In the hail of bullets that followed, Barker was shot in the legs and head, while Stamphill was struck in both legs. The other three gave up at once. Officers scrambled to the beach and retrieved the two wounded inmates. They were taken to the prison hospital where Barker died the next morning. Stamphill recovered from his wounds and was placed in isolation along with the other three captured inmates.

Two years later, the remaining four inmates were released from isolation and reassigned. During the first month after reassignment, Young, while working with McCain, stabbed McCain to death. Young received an additional three years for manslaughter. Prison officials always felt that the two inmates had bad blood between them due in part to the failed escape attempt.

Above: Dale Stamphill

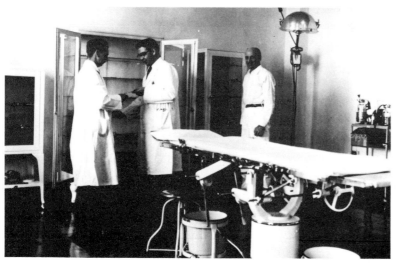

Above: The Alcatraz surgery room, where "Doc" Barker died from his wounds the following day.

Above: Henri Young

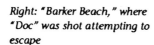

Right: "Barker Beach," where "Doc" was shot attempting to escape

ATTEMPT #5
May 21, 1941
Lloyd Barkdoll AZ#423
Arnold Kyle AZ#547
Joseph Cretzer AZ#548
Sam Shockley AZ#462

The fifth attempted escape teamed up Joseph Cretzer and Arnold Kyle, who were brothers-in-law. Cretzer was married to Kyle's sister, and both men had served time together at McNeil Federal Penitentiary. Both men were doing life as were the other two participants, Lloyd Barkdoll and Sam Shockley.

All four of the inmates had been assigned to the mat shop. On the morning of May 21, 1941, while working, they overpowered two officers and tied them up. They began trying to cut their way through a bar on one of the mat shop windows. Suddenly, Captain Madigan appeared, and he, too, was bound. After about an hour of trying to cut the bar with little success, Captain Madigan advised them to give up before someone got hurt. He reminded them that the hourly check-in by the duty officer was due in a few minutes, and without any check-in the inmates might put themselves and the officers in jeopardy. After some conversation among themselves, the four inmates decided to give up, and they untied the officers.

The four inmates were taken into custody and placed in solitary confinement or "hole" cells and later moved to the isolation cells, also in D Block.

One of the inmates, Sam Shockley, would remain in isolation until he was released by fellow inmates during the " '46 Riot."

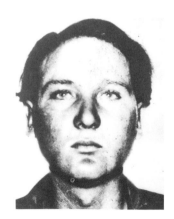

Sam Shockley

Joseph Cretzer

Arnold Kyle

Lloyd Barkdoll

ATTEMPT #6
September 15, 1941
John Bayless AZ#466

Probably the least planned and most ill-conceived escape attempt was executed by John Bayless, who was serving 25 years for bank robbery. Bayless was working on the garbage detail. Just before the final day count that ended the working day, Bayless made a dash for the water, hoping that no one would be able to find him because of the heavy fog which had engulfed the island.

Bayless scraped himself badly on the rocky shoreline. After entering the water and swimming around for a few minutes, he gave up and was pulled from the cold waters. He was taken to the prison infirmary where he was treated for cuts and bruises.

During his court hearing on the escape, Bayless tried to escape again by overpowering one of the court's bailiffs and making a run for it. He was knocked out cold by another bailiff. He was returned to Alcatraz Island and given five additional years for his second ill-fated escape attempt.

Right: Bayless after his attempted escape from court

ATTEMPT #7
April 14, 1943
Floyd Hamilton AZ#523
Fred Hunter AZ#402
James Boarman AZ#571
Harold Best AZ#380

Below: Floyd Hamilton

Below: Fred Hunter

Below: James Boarman

All four of the above inmates were assigned to an open area next to the industry building cutting cement blocks to be used with buoys for the war effort. The four inmates were serving a total of nearly 100 years plus one life sentence for various crimes ranging from bank robbery to kidnapping for ransom.

During the mid-morning hours they entered the industry building and overpowered the shop's assigned officer with knives secretly made by inmates. The officer was quickly gagged and tied up. A few minutes later, a second officer entered the shop, and he, too, was tied up and gagged. After several more minutes, the captain passed by. As soon as he noticed that the four inmates were not at their duty assignment, he entered the industry building to phone in a possible escape attempt. He, too, was taken hostage. All four men were able to escape the building by cutting through some wire mesh and breaking a shop window. They worked their way around the building out of sight of the industry tower and then headed for the water.

Just as the four inmates entered the water, one of the hostage officers managed to free himself and called in the "escape-in-progress." Immediately, Warden Johnston was notified, and the prison escape alarm began to wail for the seventh attempt in seven years.

This was the first escape my father participated in since being transferred to "The Rock." He said sometime later that this particular attempt marked the first time that prisoners tried to deal with the cold water of San Francisco Bay by greasing themselves with machine oil. They had also stolen army uniforms from the laundry and large metal containers to put them in; however, upon hearing the escape siren, they apparently abandoned the cans and began to swim away from the island.

This particular day, a friend of my father's, who had worked with him at McNeil Island Federal Prison and knew me from the time I was born, Officer Johnson, observed three of the four inmates from his model tower location. Two were swimming close together about 50 yards from the beach, while the third was closer to shore and about 20 yards further north heading towards one of the island buoys. After notifying the dock office and prison launch personnel, officer Frank Johnson fired several rounds from his .30-6 caliber rifle at all three inmates. He then took his binoculars and scanned the water. He noted that the two who were together appeared to be holding each other up, however, he was unable to spot the one who was swimming toward the buoy.

The prison launch rounded the island and proceeded to cut off the fleeing inmates. When the launch pulled alongside the two men, officers noticed that Best was holding Boarman above water, as he had been shot in the head. Best let go of Boarman in order to board the launch, and as he did so, Boarman slipped back into the water. His body was never recovered. A search for the third man in the water, Hamilton, failed. While the search for Hamilton had been going on, several officers, including my father, were checking two of the larger caves at the northwest end of the island. They found Hunter, Karpis's old partner, in one of the caves. He was taken into custody.

After talking with Officer Johnson, Warden Johnston was satisfied that Hamilton had been struck by gunfire and either died of the wound or drowned. In fact, neither had happened. Hamilton himself related his somewhat bizarre story to my father afterwards during the summer of 1943 while both were serving time in D Block, but on opposite sides of the bars.

My father remembered asking Hamilton while waiting for him to finish his once-a-week "treatment unit" shower, if the water was a little warmer than the bay water was during the escape attempt. Hamilton nodded and finished his shower. While taking Hamilton back to his cell, he told my father that Boarman and Best, after hearing the escape siren, got into the water and began swimming in a southern direction. Prior to the escape attempt, Hamilton remembered looking at a little group of rocks just off the island a couple of hundred yards. He said he must have looked at those rocks a thousand times from the shop windows. My father told him that the island kids called the rocks "Little Alcatraz." Hamilton said when he got in the water he headed for the rocks. When he arrived at "Little Alcatraz," the tide had left it two feet under water, but at least he could rest by kneeling on them. Just as he was about to turn around to see what was happening on the island, he heard a bullet whiz by his head. He ducked under water and held his breath as long as he could. He said he watched the prison launch searching near the island and the other boats out past him. Late in the afternoon the boats left. It was good timing because the tide was now down, and he could stand up out of the water when it got dark. He said he dried off in the wind and believed the machine oil he had put on before the escape had saved his life. About an hour after dark he decided to swim back to one of the caves and think about what to do next. Hamilton said that he remained in one of the caves for two days, getting battered around on the rocks by the incoming and outgoing tides. He finally retraced his escape route to the industry building and climbed in the same window he had escaped through. He said he was lucky to get back as he was cut and bruised all over from the cave. The next thing he remembered was someone shaking him awake. He looked up and saw Captain Weinhold standing over him. "As you know, they took me to the croaker (doctor), patched me up, gave me added escape attempt time, and here I am in dog block (isolation)."

My father reminded Hamilton that having been a part of the Bonnie and Clyde Gang didn't make that bay water any warmer. As he was locked down in his cell, my dad told Hamilton that Warden Johnston announced that he had died in the escape. Hamilton replied, "Mr. Hurley, I damn near did." Hamilton was returned to the general prison population five years later.

Above: "Little Alcatraz" off the northwest end of the island

ATTEMPT #8
August 7, 1943
Huron "Ted" Walters AZ#536

Below: Huron "Ted" Walters

This eighth escape attempt took place in the busiest location on Alcatraz Island during World War II, the prison laundry. Walters, who was serving 30 years for bank robbery, just walked away from the laundry building when he thought no one was looking. Unaware that he had been spotted leaving the building by a shop supervisor, Walters climbed a fence and dropped almost 40 feet to the rocky beach below. Even though Walters had been injured in his fall, he managed to tie two cans around his waist for buoyancy and got ready for his swim to freedom.

He made his way to the water's edge just as the prison escape siren sounded. He stood there unable to make up his mind whether to venture into the cold bay waters. While standing at the shore's edge, Walters was surprised by the arrival of several officers on the cliff above him ordering him to surrender. About this time the prison launch rounded the island and stood just off the shore until officers could make their way down to Walters and take him into custody.

He was taken to the prison infirmary where he was treated for cuts and bruises. He was then locked up in solitary confinement.

Right: Area near laundry where Walters dropped to the beach

ATTEMPT #9
July 31, 1945
John Giles AZ#250

John Giles was a pleasant, outgoing prisoner assigned to work in the dock area. Giles had already spent almost 10 years on "The Rock." He was under a 25-year sentence for postal robbery. Most officers felt that because Giles had accumulated nearly seven years of "good time," he would be a low risk for an escape attempt.

The author can recall even today waving to Giles as a small boy whenever the school boat returned to the island each weekday afternoon. He would always wave back.

It seemed most everyone was wrong about Giles. Over a period of time in the spring of 1945, Giles had managed to accumulate a complete army uniform that passed through the dock on its way to be cleaned. He hid the uniform on the dock until the afternoon of July 31, 1945, when he saw his opportunity.

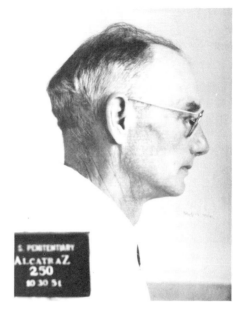

Above: John Giles

As Giles was assigned to the dock as a general cleanup man and sweeper, he virtually had the run of the area. Just before the steamship, *General Frank M. Coxe*, docked at Alcatraz, Giles removed the uniform from its hiding place on the dock, stepped between two wooden buildings, and put the uniform on beneath his prison clothing. He reappeared just as the *Coxe* was mooring at the dock, When loading was almost completed, Giles lowered himself over the end of the dock to a ledge between pilings and stripped off his prison uniform. He then stepped onto the lower deck of the *Coxe*, unnoticed, just as she was about to get under way. Because Giles was changing when the *Coxe* arrived at the dock, he could not have noticed from which direction the ship had approached the island, but he merely assumed that it would be heading for San Francisco. He realized his mistake too late when he watched helplessly as the *Coxe* pointed her bow towards Angel Island Army Post.

The *Coxe* had not traveled more than a couple of hundred yards from the island when a dock prisoner count revealed that Giles was missing. Associate Warden Miller was notified at once. He, along with two other officers, boarded the prison launch and headed for Angel Island. The officers arrived at Angel Island nearly five minutes ahead of the *Coxe* and were waiting for Giles as he walked down the gangway in his army uniform, which had sergeant chevrons on the sleeves. He was immediately taken into custody, shackled hand and foot, and returned to Alcatraz.

The author and a friend were walking along the lower balcony, which overlooked the dock, that day when we observed the prison launch heading towards Alcatraz from Angel Island. As neither of us had seen this happening before, we asked the dock tower officer what had happened, because no prison escape siren had sounded during this attempt. The tower officer told us that Giles had tried to escape on the *Coxe*. We waited for the prison launch to arrive. After it had docked in the boat slip, a heavily shackled Giles, still in army uniform, got off the launch flanked by two officers and followed by Associate Warden Miller. Just for a moment, Giles looked up at my friend and me standing on the balcony. He was quickly escorted to a waiting truck and whisked away towards the prison. Though neither one of us said anything, I am sure we both felt that somehow we had lost a friend that day. He had always smiled at all us kids and waved.

Although I never saw Giles again, my father told me that for his trouble, Giles lost all his good time, spent four years in isolation, and was given five additional years for the attempted escape.

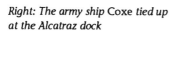

Right: The army ship Coxe *tied up at the Alcatraz dock*

ATTEMPT #10
May 2, 1946 (The Alcatraz Riot)
Joseph Cretzer AZ#548
Bernard Coy AZ#415
Marvin Hubbard AZ#645
Miran Thompson AZ#729
Sam (Crazy Sam) Shockley AZ#462
Clarence Carnes AZ#714

Joseph Cretzer

May 2, 1946 ushered in the two bloodiest days of Alcatraz Island's 29-year history as a federal penitentiary. There were six participants in this attempted escape, which was ill-organized and ended in a tragic blood bath for inmates and officers alike.

Those involved were Joseph Cretzer, Bernard Coy, Marvin Hubbard, Miran Thompson, Sam Shockley, and Clarence Carnes. They were desperate men who collectively were serving more than 270 years along with three life sentences.

The inmates' plan was put into action just after 1:30 p.m., while most of the inmate population was away from the cellhouse working. Coy, who had been assigned the task of mopping in the cell house, bided his time until one of the kitchen cleanup inmates, Hubbard, approached the dining room entrance where Officer William Miller was waiting to search him. Miller was the only officer at this time in the main cell house proper and, as per policy, was unarmed.

Bernard Coy

There were, however, two other officers in Miller's immediate area. Officer Burt Burch was assigned to the west gun gallery, a multi-leveled passageway that runs east-west at the north end of the cell house. The gallery, located just over the dining hall entrance, was separated from the D Block by a steel door just as D Block was separated from the rest of the main cell house. As the gallery is enclosed by steel bars and wire mesh, Burch was armed with a .45-caliber automatic and a .30-caliber rifle. The other officer in the area was Thomas Corwin, who was assigned to D Block or isolation. He was separated from the main cell house by a steel door. Corwin, too, was unarmed.

Marvin Hubbard

When Coy hit the echoing steel cell house with his bucket full of water, it was a cue for inmate Shockley, who had been locked up in D Block since an attempted 1941 escape, to begin causing a disturbance. He began throwing things out of his cell, yelling, screaming, and generally creating a commotion. Officer Corwin called Burch in the

Miran Thompson

Sam Shockley

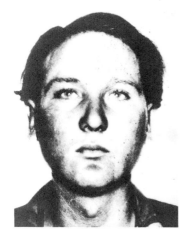

Clarence Carnes

gallery and asked if he would walk through the passageway to D Block and "stand by" till Corwin could check on Shockley.

After the door had closed behind Burch as he entered D Block, Miller, who was now completely alone in the main cell house, was jumped by Coy and Hubbard. Officer Miller was choked so hard by Coy that he fell into unconsciousness. The two inmates dragged Miller to an open unoccupied cell (403) where he was tied and gagged. The adjacent cell (402) was also open and vacant. (Refer to sketch on page 32.) After taking all of Miller's keys, overlooking a loose one in his pocket (key 107), Coy and Hubbard began unlocking the lever boxes that controlled the levers which opened all the cell doors in B and C Blocks. This allowed inmates Cretzer, Thompson, and Carnes to join them. Coy now went to his cell and retrieved an inmate-crafted bar spreader he had made several months before. He had hidden it in his toilet disassembled, and it was made to look like plumbing.

Coy stripped to his shorts and greased himself with lard from the kitchen. He then climbed the three-story gun gallery to a point near the top where the bars go from vertical to an almost horizontal position to fasten into the wall. Coy took the spreader and placed it between the bars and turned them. Within a matter of minutes, he had spread the bars far enough to allow him to squeeze through and drop to the gallery floor. He quickly made his way to the gallery door which separated the part of the passageway that overlooked D Block from that which overlooked B and C Blocks. Coy climbed the wire mesh and took up a position just above the door where he waited for Officer Burch to return from D Block. Within a couple of minutes, Burch did return, and as he stepped through the door, Coy dropped down on him, knocking Burch to the passageway floor. Coy then grabbed the rifle that Burch had dropped. Burch quickly regained his footing and a struggle ensued. Coy struck Burch in the face with the butt of the rifle, leaving him dazed. Inmate Coy quickly grabbed Burch by the necktie, pulling it tight, and he held on until Burch slipped into unconsciousness.

Coy then removed Burch's .45-caliber automatic along with all the keys, ammo, gas mask, and billy clubs he could lay his hands on, and passed the ill-gotten booty down to Cretzer and others. He kept the rifle for himself. Coy next moved through the gallery passage door into the area that overlooks D Block. With his rifle pointed at

Left: West gun gallery where Coy climbed to spread the bars

Corwin, Coy ordered him to open the steel door that leads from D Block to the main cell house. When the unarmed Corwin unlocked and opened the door, Cretzer pushed his way through. Cretzer pointed the .45-caliber automatic at Corwin and ordered him to lay face down on the floor. Shockley was released at this time. However, Cretzer was unable to release his old friend "Whitey" Franklin from his #9 solitary confinement cell, as an electronic override could not be bridged to free him. Franklin was in solitary for his part in the failed 1938 attempt to escape in which Officer Royal Cline had been killed.

Corwin was then taken to cell 403 where he was tossed in with Miller. The six would-be escapees were now in control of most of the cell house. It was time to make their move. Their goal was to leave the cell house by way of the door which led to the prison yard. Next they wanted to capture the road tower with its weapons and, with enough hostages, make their getaway using the prison launch. The first step, however, was to unlock the cell house door leading to the prison yard. Coy, armed with all the keys he could get his hands on, tried them all. To his dismay and anger, none of the keys would open the door. Believing

Officer Miller had the key to their freedom, the six convicts raced to cell 403. Normally key 107 would have been returned to the west gun gallery before Miller had eaten lunch, but on this particular day, he had forgotten to return the key. When Corwin was put in the cell with Miller, he removed his gag for a minute. Miller, who was conscious by now, told Corwin to take the key and put it down the toilet as both were aware what might happen if the six escapees got out of the cell house proper. Corwin returned the gag to Miller's mouth before the convicts got to the cell. They took the gag out of Miller's mouth and began beating and kicking him, yelling for him to give them the right key that would open the yard door. Unconscious again, Miller was returned to his cell.

The next officer to be taken hostage was Robert Bristow, a steward, who had entered the main cell house from the kitchen. He was taken hostage immediately and put in the same cell as Officers Miller and Corwin. In quick succession, Captain Henry Weinhold, Lieutenant Joe Simpson, and Officers John Baker, "Sunny" Sundstrom, Joe Burdett, and Ernest Lageson were jumped and taken hostage as they entered the cell house over a 20-minute period to ascertain why phones within the cell house were not being answered. All were put in cell 403 except Baker, Sundstrom, and Simpson. They were held in cell 402.

At 2:20 p.m. Officer Clifford Fish, who was assigned to the armory on this day, had been unsuccessful in reaching any of the officers who had entered the cell house in order to ascertain if there was any trouble. He finally contacted Associate Warden Ed Miller and informed him that several officers, including the captain, had entered the cell house sometime earlier, but had failed to return.

Associate Warden Miller grabbed a gas billy (no firearms were allowed within the cell house) and entered the cell house between B and C Blocks, sometimes called "Broadway." Miller could hear nothing as he proceeded down "Broadway." All of a sudden, Coy stepped out from the cutoff and took aim at Miller with his rifle. As Miller turned to run he accidentally hit the gas billy on an overhead walkway tier and it discharged, striking the right side of his face. As he ran towards the main cell house entrance, he could feel a bullet whiz by his ear. After escaping through the door, he immediately notified Warden Johnston that Coy was loose within the cell house with a rifle, and he could not determine the fate of several officers who had more than likely been taken hostage by whoever was involved.

Warden Johnston sent Miller to a temporary first aid station to have the burn on the right side of his face taken care of. Warden Johnston ordered that the prison siren be sounded and that all off-duty and day-off officers report to the prison administration immediately.

As soon as the escape siren began its long uphill wail notifying most everyone in the Bay Area that once more an escape was in progress on "The Rock," the six involved inmates knew that their chances for a successful breakout were all but over. Earlier, Coy had returned to cell 403 to re-check Miller and the other hostages for the key to open the prison yard door. After searching all the hostages, he checked the toilet and recovered key 107 where Corwin had hidden it upon Miller's suggestion. Coy tried it in the yard door, but by then the lock was too chewed up for any key to fit in it, thus leaving the six inmates confined within the cell house walls.

After the escape siren began sounding, Coy took Burch's rifle to the dining hall window and fired at the officer in the hill tower, striking him in the leg. Coy also took a shot at the dock tower officer, but fortunately missed. About this time Cretzer took the .45 caliber Coy had taken off Officer Burch and went to one of the D Block windows. Cretzer could observe several officers on the sloping hill on the west side of the prison. The author's father happened to be one of those officers. Cretzer began shooting indiscriminately at them. As my father ducked behind a large boulder, he heard a bullet whiz over the top of his head and another two in quick succession strike the stone. One of the two bullets chipped a piece of the boulder, which flew up and grazed his right temple. After the shoot-

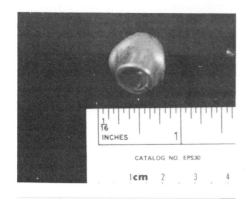

Above: Two slugs that were recovered after being fired at my father

ing stopped, my father took his pocket knife and recovered both bullet slugs by digging them out from the base of the rock.

The hostage officers were not so fortunate. By now the six convicts were in a panic. Shockley and Thompson began yelling at Cretzer, "Kill all of the bastards. We don't want to leave any witnesses who can finger us and shove us in the gas chamber." After hearing this over and over, Cretzer put a fresh clip into the .45 automatic and walked over to the front of hostage cell 403.

Captain Weinhold stood up at the front of the cell. He advised Cretzer to put down the gun and give himself up. Cretzer replied, "If anyone gets it, you will be the first son-of-a-bitch to go." Shockley and Thompson continued to egg Cretzer on. Cretzer finally obliged. He pointed the gun directly into the cell and began firing. Captain Weinhold was struck in the chest and arm. Officer Miller, still unconscious, was struck in the arm. After the clip was empty, Cretzer moved to the next hostage cell, cell 402, while putting a fresh clip in the automatic. Again egged on by Shockley, Thompson, and now even Coy, Cretzer continued the carnage. He fired point blank into the cell striking Lieutenant Simpson in the chest and upper abdomen and hit Officer Baker twice in the leg. Officer Sundstrom, who was the third officer in cell 402, fell when Cretzer began firing, but was uninjured and played dead. Although there were six officers in cell 403, Bristow and Burdett were uninjured. Officer Lageson received a slight wound to the jaw and, like the other officers who were conscious, played dead. While lying on the cell floor, he retrieved a pencil from his pocket and wrote down the names of the six inmates involved on the cell wall.

By now, inmates Carnes, Thompson, and even Shockley had decided to return to their respective cells, hoping that all the hostages were dead so that no one would be able to tie them directly to the attempted escape. Coy, Cretzer, and Hubbard, however, had already decided that if they were going to die, they were going to take as many of the officers with them as possible. Cretzer then climbed to the top of C Block, while Coy remained on "Seedy Street," on the west side of C Block. They both took up positions at the two locations.

Several hours later, Lieutenant Phil Bergen led a team into the west gun gallery in order to rescue Officer Burch if, in fact, he was still alive. Upon entering the gallery, the officers immediately received fire from the cell house floor on

Alcatraz Island: Maximum Security

"Seedy Street" and the top of C Block. As Officer Stites raised himself somewhat to return the fire, he was hit several times and died almost instantly.* Officers Herschel Oldham, Harry Cochran, and Fred Richberger were also struck by gunfire. Officer Burch was rescued, and the wounded officers, along with Stites, were removed to safety. Lt. Bergen and the remaining officers then positioned themselves along the lower catwalk of the gallery where an open phone line was maintained with the prison armory.

Shortly after midnight on May 3, Lieutenants Ike Faulk and Fred Roberts entered the cell house in search of the hostage officers. Each lieutenant had a team of five volunteers. It was a dangerous mission as Warden Johnston had previously ordered all the lights off in the main cell house. His policy of no firearms inside the cell house was still enforced as the fate of the hostages had still not been determined. The volunteers were armed only with gas billys, while each lieutenant carried a flashlight. Lt. Roberts and his group edged their way down "Broadway" between B and C Blocks in the dark. As Roberts turned on his flashlight in order to check cells, his team immediately came under fire from Cretzer, who was above them on top of C Block. Lt. Roberts was struck twice in the legs. His team members quickly pulled Roberts out of the line of fire. As soon as Cretzer began firing on Roberts and his team, Lt. Bergen, who was in the west gun gallery with his team, began spraying the top of C Block with machine gun fire and every other weapon they had. Cretzer, though, was hidden behind a cement column. The only way he would be struck by a bullet would be one that ricocheted off something. Lt. Faulk and his team had better luck. They discovered the hostages on "Seedy Street" in cells 402 and 403. Fortunately for Faulk and his team, Coy and Hubbard had retreated to the passageway which runs between the cells in C Block. Lt. Faulk used the manual cell door override to open the cell doors and removed all the hostages to safety. All of the hostage officers were alive when rescued; however, Miller died at the Marine Hospital in San Francisco several hours later as a result of beatings and a gunshot wound inflicted by his captors.

*Note: It was never determined just who was responsible for Officer Stites' death; however, it is generally believed that during the confusion of entering the gallery and receiving inmate gunfire, Officer Stites may have died from friendly gunfire as well as inmate gunfire when he stood up to return fire.

Above: Dock officer warning press representatives to move out further from the island

Right: San Francisco Chronicle's account of the riot

Alcatraz Island: Maximum Security

Above: As the battle rages on Alcatraz, armed officers on the roof keep watch as officers below fire rocket grenades.

Late Friday night on May 3 the U.S. Marines began dropping concussion grenades through holes they had drilled in the cell house roof. The grenades forced Cretzer to leave his perch on top of C Block and descend to floor level inside the passageway between east and west C Block. There he ran into Coy and Hubbard.

Just before dawn, a small group of officers under Associate Warden Miller positioned themselves along the passageway of the east gun gallery. Twice these officers reported muffled talking coming from the passageway in C Block.

As dawn arrived on Saturday, May 4, Warden Johnston decided since the hostages had been safely removed from the cell house, it was time to end the bloody insurrection by retaking control of the cell house. A team of officers

quietly entered the south main entrance to the cell house—this time with weapons. They proceeded to the C Block passageway door. When the command was given, the door was opened, and a burst of machine gun fire sprayed the darkened corridor. The door was then quickly shut. Thirty seconds went by without any return fire, so the door was again opened and the procedure was repeated. A couple of minutes later, officers entered the passageway and found the three inmates dead. It appeared that Coy and Cretzer had died sometime during the night as their bodies were cold. Several bullet holes were observed in each of their bodies; however, both men still had weapons in their hands. Hubbard was found further back in the passageway. It appeared that he had been dead only a short while as his body was still warm to the touch. Hubbard also had several bullet holes in him. All three inmates also had pieces of grenade fragments in them.

As the bodies were being removed from the passageway, Associate Warden Ed Miller commented to another officer, "Well, it looks like these three bastards made good their escape, even if it was done feet first."

Below: From l. to r. the bodies of Bernard Coy, Joseph Cretzer, and Marvin Hubbard in the utility corridor

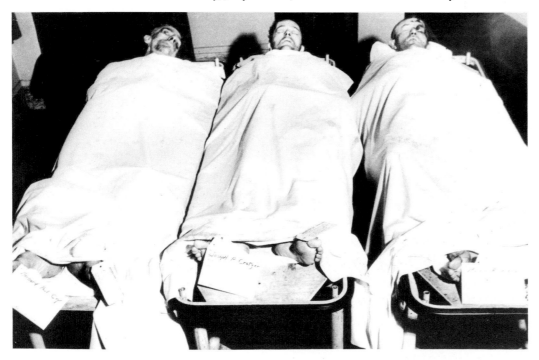

Alcatraz Island: Maximum Security

After 42 hours the carnage on Alcatraz Island was finally over.

THE TOLL: Two officers dead
Fifteen officers wounded
Three inmates dead
One inmate wounded

The three remaining inmates were quickly rounded up and placed in the "hole." After their arraignments in federal court, all three were placed in isolation cells to await trial on several counts, including the murder of Officer William Miller. Over a year later, all three were convicted of the first degree murder of Miller. Both Shockley and Thompson were sentenced to death in San Quentin's gas chamber, while Carnes was given 99 years tacked onto the life sentence he was already serving. Both Shockley and Thompson were transferred to San Quentin's death row to await execution. Carnes was returned to Alcatraz where he would spend the next seven years in isolation cell #41. During the month of December 1948, Shockley and Thompson paid their debt to society in the gas chamber just two and one-half years after the end of the " '46 Riot."

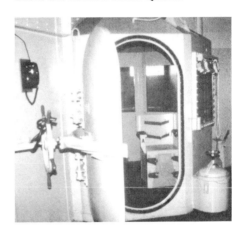

Below: Gas chamber at San Quentin

Officer Harold Stites died as a result of gunfire, friendly or otherwise, while attempting to rescue Officer Burt Burch from the west gun gallery.

Officer William Miller died as a result of severe beatings and a gunshot wound by inmates while being held a hostage.

Two of the wounded hostage officers, Captain Henry Weinhold and Lieutenant Joe Simpson, had been wounded so severely that they retired on disability.

Warden James A. Johnston retired in April of 1948 and was appointed to serve on the U.S. Board of Parole. He lived in San Francisco until his death in 1958.

Associate Warden Ed Miller retired shortly after the " '46 Riot." He returned to his native Kansas where he died shortly thereafter.

Carnes was transferred from Alcatraz two months before the prison closed in March 1963. He was sent to the medical facility at Springfield, Missouri, due to health reasons, and then on to Leavenworth Penitentiary. He was paroled in 1973 and returned to prison twice after that, once to get medical treatment. Carnes finally died of kidney failure in October 1988 at the Springfield facility.

Although Warden Johnston felt that there were many things that could have been done in a different manner, he did, shortly after the riot, comment on his officers' bravery. He stated, "All his officers did their duty to a man."

Right: Warden Johnston views one of the hostage cells after the bloody riot.

Above: Bodies of Cretzer, Coy, and Hubbard taken off prison launch at Pier 4 in San Francisco

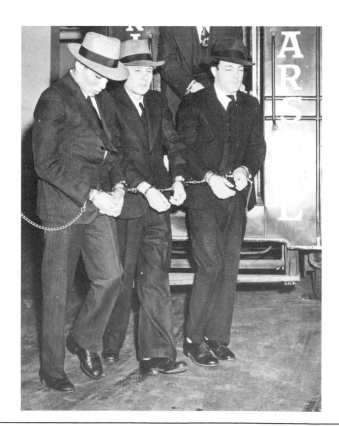

Right: Thompson, Shockley, and Carnes enroute to the federal court building for arraignment

Alcatraz Island: Maximum Security

ATTEMPT #11
July 23, 1956
Floyd P. Wilson AZ#956

Floyd P. Wilson was serving a life sentence for murder. During the summer months of 1956, he was assigned to the dock area moving cargo around the dock and making bundles secure with sash cord for shipment from the island. He had earlier taken several feet of this sash cord and hidden it on the dock in order to prepare for the first attempt to escape from the island since the ill-fated escape riot of 1946.

Floyd P. Wilson

Wilson's plan seemed simple enough. He waited until late afternoon. When he thought that no one was watching, he walked in a slow, easy fashion to the south end of the dock where several large boulders are located just below the sea wall. After wrapping the sash cord around his waist, Wilson quickly slipped over the sea wall and concealed himself between two huge boulders until dark. The plan was to find some driftwood, tie the pieces together to form a raft, and float his way to freedom.

Within minutes of his concealment, Wilson's absence was discovered, and the prison siren, which had been silent for many years, once more began its eerie wail. A search party was quickly organized with the dock area being the focal point for the hunt. Wilson remained concealed between the rocks for several hours. He then felt that he must get further away from the dock area, so he came out of hiding and began edging his way southeast along the sea wall.

At about midnight, while searching on the beach for some driftwood to lash together, he was spotted by officers and at once ordered to surrender. After 11 hours of evading detection, Wilson was taken into custody, returned to the cell house, and placed in solitary confinement.

Right: Area southeast of dock where Wilson hid from officers during his ill-fated attempt

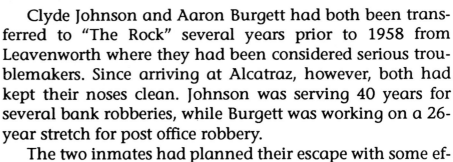

ATTEMPT #12
September 29, 1958
Aaron Burgett AZ#991
Clyde Johnson AZ#864

Aaron Burgett

Clyde Johnson

Clyde Johnson and Aaron Burgett had both been transferred to "The Rock" several years prior to 1958 from Leavenworth where they had been considered serious troublemakers. Since arriving at Alcatraz, however, both had kept their noses clean. Johnson was serving 40 years for several bank robberies, while Burgett was working on a 26-year stretch for post office robbery.

The two inmates had planned their escape with some effort. They had greased themselves for the cold bay water and had even made crude face masks and snorkels. In addition, Burgett had made a pair of wood swim fins for his feet.

Both men had been assigned to the garbage truck detail for several months. On this particular day, while working near the south end of the island outside the security fence near the family housing, the two men overpowered the detail officer, H. Miller. They dragged him over to the south area of the island where the cliff slopes more gently to the water's edge. Officer Miller was then gagged and tied to a tree.

The two inmates then raced down to the beach and made their way along the rocky shore on the southwest side of the island. Johnson watched his escape partner slip into the water and disappear. Johnson, however, was having problems of his own. As he stood there knee deep in the icy bay waters, he realized that if he tried to make a swim for it, his chances of making it would be about zero. Johnson decided to return to the rocky beach and attempted to hide there.

Within half an hour Officer Miller was discovered, and prison officials were notified. At once the prison siren was activated, and a massive search by prison personnel and Coast Guard boats got underway. It took the Coast Guard nearly two hours of circling the island before they found Johnson concealed in some rocks near the water's edge. Prison officers were notified; they responded and took Johnson into custody.

The search for Burgett, however, proved negative. It seems as though he had just vanished. The search for Burgett became nationwide.

If prison officials had only known that all they had to do was just wait! Two weeks to the day after the escape, the unpredictable San Francisco Bay had decided to give up Burgett. His body surfaced less than the distance of a block from the island and was spotted by the road tower officer. The prison launch was summoned to retrieve him. Even though Burgett was still wearing the makeshift wooden swim fins on his feet, it took fingerprints to establish his identity as his body was decomposed.

It almost seems that San Francisco Bay was once again sending a message to potential escapees: "If you are going to successfully escape from Alcatraz Island, you must first get by me."

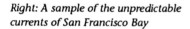

Right: A sample of the unpredictable currents of San Francisco Bay

ATTEMPT #13
June 11, 1962 ("Escape From Alcatraz")
Frank Morris AZ#1441
Clarence Anglin AZ#1485
John Anglin AZ#1476
Allen West AZ#1335

FRANK LEE MORRIS, DOB 9-1-26, age 35, Ht- 5'7¼", Wt-135 lbs., eyes hazel, hair black, build regular, tattoo: Devil's head upper R.arm; star on each knee, star on left knee with 7 above 11 below; star base L. thumb, 13 base of L. index finger.

Frank Morris

JOLLN WILLIAM ANGLIN, DOB 5-2-30, age 32, Ht 5'10", Wt- 140 lbs., eyes blue, hair blonde, build medium, small scar on left side of cheek, round scar on left side of forearm.

John Anglin

The so-called "Escape from Alcatraz" was an idea originally hatched by Allen West. He was one of the few inmates to have served time on "The Rock" twice. His first incarceration on the island was from 1954 till 1956. His second time was from 1958 till 1963 when the prison closed. West was in his early thirties the second time around and was on a 10-year stretch for several interstate transportation convictions.

In 1961 he was released from isolation in D Block after serving several months, along with other prisoners, for cutting their heel tendons in a protest over mental abuse by prison authorities. West's wounds were of a minor nature, and he had no lasting effects from the incident.

When he was returned to the main prison population, West was assigned to general maintenance duties inside the main cell house. Day after day as he was sweeping, scrubbing, and painting, West could not help but notice how the inside of the prison structure was deteriorating. He observed cracks in the walls, floors, and even within the cells themselves.[1] At night he began checking his own cell and found that it was fairly easy to chip away small pieces of cement around the heating vent at the rear of his cell.[2] By this time an escape was becoming a real possibility for West and he almost became obsessed with looking for avenues out of the aging prison.

West decided that it was time to bring in some of the other inmates to begin planning for an escape. He contacted John and Clarence Anglin, two brothers with whom West had served time at a Florida prison several years before.

Both Anglin brothers had been transferred from Atlanta Penitentiary to Alcatraz after several escape attempts. The brothers were serving long terms for bank robbery.

---

1 Small cracks were noticed in floors and on walls shortly after the " '46 Riot" because of fragment grenades used to regain the cell house.

2 When the cell house was upgraded in 1934, the vents were made smaller, but not reinforced.

Alcatraz Island: Maximum Security

Frank Morris, who was another fairly recent arrival at Alcatraz, had served time with the Anglins at Atlanta for a number of crimes, including bank robbery. He was the fourth man brought into the escape scheme.

Each of the four inmates checked the rear of his cell. They all discovered that the cement around the vents chipped away fairly easily. The men now had a way to get out of their cells. The escape plan was put into operation in December 1961. Each was given his assignment. First, they began chipping at the cement around the heat vents with filed-down spoons, metal scraps, and any other tools they could devise. They covered their work from prison officers by making fake vents surrounded by cardboard that looked like the cement adjacent to the vent grills. *Papiermaché* heads were also made out of chips of cement, cardboard, toilet paper, and hair from the barber shop. It has been estimated that from 10 to 20 inmates were involved in supplying materials for the attempted escape.

After completing two of the dummy heads and having completed two holes through the heat vents which led to the utility corridor, the escape plan was ready to enter its second phase.

West, whose general maintenance job was the perfect cover, convinced officials that the top of C Block tier needed to be scraped and painted. He even got officials to have a number of blankets strung around the top of the tier so chips would not fall onto the cell house floor.

Morris and John Anglin could now put the dummy heads in their bunks as soon as the lights were turned out at 9:30 p.m. Then they removed the fake vents and crawled into the utility corridor. They would then replace the vents, climb the three stories to the top of B Block tier, and fashion the items needed for their escape. Their efforts were masked by the blankets strung around the tier.

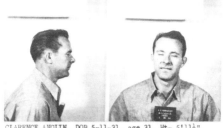

CLARENCE ANGLIN, DOB 5-11-31, age 31, Ht- 5'11½", Wt- 168 lbs., build medium, eyes hazel, comp. light, tattoo: "Zona" left wrist; "Nita" right 4 arm.

Clarence Anglin

The four prisoners by now had assembled raincoats, a homemade flashlight, prison-made chisels, and four hacksaw blades which had been hidden in a cell door jamb since 1945. West supplied a type of epoxy from the paint shop to use as an adhesive for the raincoats which were to be made into a raft. While one inmate completed a 7-foot by 14-foot raft (according to West), the others used hacksaw blades to cut through bolts that held a ceiling vent in place which led to the prison's roof.

For almost six incredible months they continued undetected to fashion items for the escape. The thing that took so long was cutting through the roof vent. They could not afford to make too much noise nor spend an excessive amount of time out of their cells each night.

The fateful day finally arrived on June 11, 1962. Everything was ready. The four men decided to leave just after the last stand-up count in front of the bars at 9:30 p.m. After this count and when the lights were turned out, Morris, West, and the Anglin brothers put their plan into action. First, they put the dummy heads in their bunks along with rolled blankets to give the appearance they were sleeping. Next, they removed the phony vents and crawled through into the passageway. The vents were then replaced. At this point, something went wrong. West was

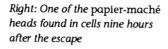

Right: One of the papier-maché heads found in cells nine hours after the escape

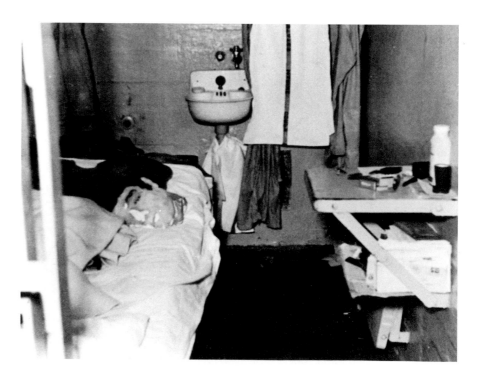

unable to remove the vent from the rear of his cell. It appeared that the cement-type epoxy which held his vent in place would not budge, preventing West from having access to the passageway.

The other three men could not wait for West to get free from his cell. They climbed the three cell block tiers to reach the open space just below the prison roof. It is believed that they then knocked the ventilator fan cover off, the one they cut through, and climbed out onto the prison roof. During the next phase of the plan, they lowered themselves down a prison building drain pipe, climbed a fence, and made their way toward the water. There the three inmates blew up the makeshift raft of raincoats with the bellows from Morris's concertina. They then apparently entered the water and have never been seen since.

By now, West, who was still back stranded in his cell, had decided that his chances for an escape were now gone. He recalled later that he spent the night lying in his bunk waiting for morning and the inevitable spotlight that would focus on him.

The escape was not discovered until early on the morning of June 12, some nine hours after the three inmates had left their cells. The discovery was made when an officer was unable to wake up Morris. The officer opened his cell, and the dummy head which had been counted all night by officers, rolled off the bunk and onto the cell floor when the covers were pulled back.

It was determined within a few minutes that three inmates were missing. A complete lock-down of the prison was ordered, while officers scrambled around in an attempt to ascertain just how the three escapees had gotten out of the cell house. West finally yelled at one of the officers and motioned for him to step over to his cell. He confessed to the officer that he had been involved in the escape and had, in fact, been its major planner.

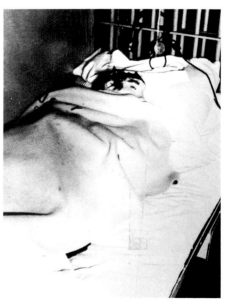

West, after being segregated from the main cell house for interrogation, revealed to officials that the escape route included making their way to the eastern tip of Angel Island, stealing a boat, and then heading for the Marin County coastline. Once ashore the escapees would break into a store for guns, clothes, and other supplies. They would then steal a car and head north.

Right: One of the dummy heads counted by officers during the night

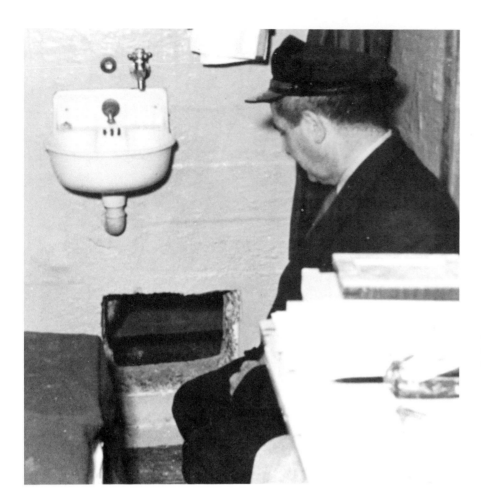

Left: Officer views one of three holes at rear of cells which allowed inmates to flee prison.

Right: Dummy heads made of papier-maché to fool officers during an escape attempt

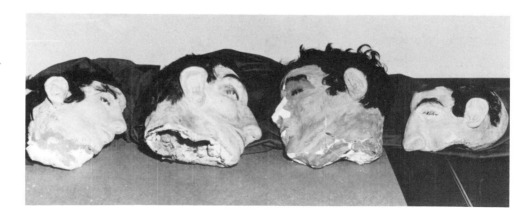

The search started with Alcatraz Island. On the roof, officers found a small raft made out of raincoats; however, West contended that a much larger one had been taken by the three men. (Note: No trace of a larger raft was ever found.) Over the next few days, several items were recovered by authorities and private persons. A couple found a makeshift life jacket identical to one left on the prison roof the night of the escape. A paddle was also found. Also recovered a couple of days later was a watertight plastic bag containing several letters to friends of the Anglin brothers as well as a number of photos. There was also a $10 money order made out to Anglin. This bag was recovered by a patrol boat between Angel Island and the Golden Gate Bridge, just off the Marin County shore. It is not likely that if all had gone well, this item would have been left behind. After a search of the San Francisco Bay Area with negative results, it was expanded to a nationwide hunt.

There are several points to be made in regards to the success or failure of this most famous escape attempt from "The Rock." Yes, I would call it an unsuccessful escape for several reasons. Here are some:

1. *The water current was running outbound at eight knots, or nine miles per hour, at the time of the attempt.*

2. *With water temperatures in San Francisco averaging 53°F, hypothermia became a serious threat to anyone not protected by a wet suit and experienced in the art of cold water swimming. The three escapees had neither.*

3. *It seems very unlikely that three men, who had spent more than half their lives in one type of prison or another, would never be heard from again in more than 27 years.*

Not long after the prison closed in March 1963, the author visited a friend who also grew up on Alcatraz Island. This friend's father had retired when the prison closed and became the caretaker of the island for the Department of General Services that had charge of the island until 1970.

My friend and I examined the entire escape route taken by Morris and the Anglins. Three things became apparent at once:

1. *The inmates had a lot of help and support from other prisoners while planning the escape, although West never did name anyone else.*

2. *Months of work by the inmates, such as chipping, sawing, and the stealing of materials, would not have gone unnoticed for such an extended period of time.*

3. *Finally, the most puzzling item of all. The three escapees were not seen on the roof by the officer in #2 road tower, which was always manned on a 24-hour basis.*

Several years after visiting my friend, I believe that the tower mystery was solved. I talked with two officers and two inmates who were on the island at the time of the Morris-Anglin attempt. Both inmates related that the tower was not manned during the evening hours, while only one officer stated for sure that the tower was shut down during the evening hours by June 1962, due in part to officer cutbacks. The second officer was not sure about the status of the road tower.

If only one conclusion can be drawn from the Morris-Anglin attempted escape, it would be that the once ultramaximum-security penitentiary at Alcatraz Island had slipped to become a tired, old correctional facility, which by the late 1950s was resting on her laurels as the once "escape-proof" prison. It appears that cutbacks in officer personnel, training, and a deteriorating facility all lent themselves to this uncharacteristic event called "The Escape from Alcatraz."

ATTEMPT #14
December 16, 1962
John P. Scott AZ#1403
Darl Lee Parker AZ#1413

The final escape attempt took place late on a Sunday afternoon. John Paul Scott was serving 30 years for bank robbery, while Darl Parker was doing 50 years for the same type of offense. Both inmates had been assigned to the kitchen for the past 18 months, and for nearly a year both had been working on loosening a couple of bars to a storeroom window. Their tools consisted of butcher's twine soaked in wax and covered with scouring cleanser and a serrated spatula. Items that had been stolen over the long, prepared escape included several pairs of rubber medical gloves that were to be used for flotation once the men gained access to the water.

John Paul Scott

During the late afternoon of December 16, 1962, the two inmates had succeeded in moving the bar far enough to allow them to squeeze through the small opening and exit the prison. The two men now waited for the final kitchen count of the day. When that was completed they greased themselves with lard stolen from the kitchen and squeezed through the bars. Once outside they climbed to the roof by way of a drain pipe, crossed over to the east side of the prison roof, and lowered themselves to the ground with an electrical cord previously stolen.

They both knew at this point that they were in the most exposed position of the entire escape: next to the road that leads to the warden's house and in front of the prison administration offices. They quickly made their way to a shrub-covered area near the base of the water tower. Next they eased cautiously down a small hill, crossed over the roadway which led to the industry area, and made their way to the power house, located near the cliffs just above the water. Parker related later that only five minutes had passed since leaving the prison, but it seemed more like five hours. The freedom seekers next moved slowly along the northeast shoreline of the island until they had arrived at a point just below the fog horn. Both men had just completed inflating several pairs of stolen medical gloves when the escape siren began the final ear-splitting wail of its 29-year history. Scott and Parker quickly stuffed the inflated gloves into their pants and shirts and entered the water. Immediately the Coast Guard was notified and, along with both prison launches, began to circle the island. Parker got

Darl Lee Parker

as far as a group of rocks, about 200 feet off the northwest end of the island. (Refer to page 93.) As earlier stated, the rocks were referred to as "Little Alcatraz" by the island's children. As soon as officers from one of the prison launches spotted him, he gave up. On boarding the launch, Parker declared that the water was too cold, and the water current was moving too fast. He felt that to continue would have meant drowning. Scott, however, was nowhere to be found.

Nearly an hour after Parker had been taken into custody, the prison armory received a call. Scott AZ#403 was in custody and under guard by the military police at Letterman General Hospital, the U.S. Army hospital at the Presidio.

It appeared that the swift current, aided by the inflated medical gloves, carried Scott to a point on the rocks just below Fort Point. Scott, who was barely coherent, was found by two boys who notified the military police. Scott's condition was very serious. He was suffering from extreme hypothermia and shock.

A detail of officers were dispatched from Alcatraz to stand guard over Scott until he was well enough to be returned to Alcatraz. Had inmate Scott been carried only as far as one block north of the rocks he ended upon, his body would have been carried out to sea, and its chances for recovery would have been just about nil. Scott's escape attempt was unique in one respect. He could boast of being the only prisoner ever to reach the mainland and live to tell about it. However, like the first escape attempt by John Bowers in 1936 and the other 12 in between, all were destined to fail.

On March 21, 1963, the federal penitentiary at Alcatraz Island closed its doors, and all the inmates were transferred to other federal prisons. Scott and Parker were removed from isolation and also transferred.

Above: Scott and Parker enroute to court after escape attempt

Following Page: Escape route taken by inmates Scott and Parker during the last escape attempt from "The Rock"

Alcatraz Island: Maximum Security

THE INTERVIEW: FORMER INMATE REVEALS HIS LIFE OF CRIME

Ex-con Describes the Hell of Incarceration at Alcatraz and Tells It Like It Was

While researching this chapter, the author was fortunate to have been able to interview three ex-inmates who had served time on Alcatraz Island. Two of these men served time when my father had worked on "The Rock." The third man was incarcerated on the island during its last few years as a federal prison. All the interviews took place between June and November 1988. Having been in law enforcement for many years, the author was able, with the help of some friends who shall remain anonymous, to locate two ex-inmates for the interviews.

After weighing the three interviews carefully, I chose the ex-inmate who I felt would give the best insight as to the "how" and "why" a man would end up serving time on Alcatraz Island. One of these men offered information that would best allow the reader to capture the penetrating feeling I had during my interview. For purposes of this interview, I shall refer to this man as Nick Baxter.

Having received information that an Alcatraz ex-inmate had been living in the Southern California area since 1966, I decided to go there to talk to him. On a Saturday morning, prior to leaving the airport, I called Nick Baxter at his barber shop. When I was sure I had Baxter on the phone, I advised him that I was writing a book on Alcatraz and would like to interview him. He seemed surprised that I had found him. Baxter said nothing for what seemed like an eternity. Then he told me that his past was behind him, and he wanted to leave it that way. After a considerable amount of my pleading, Baxter agreed but with certain conditions. He told me that I could not record the interview, use his real name, or use any prison numbers or specific years of incarceration. I asked him to reconsider on a couple of points, but he told me that was the only way he would be interviewed. After I finally agreed, Baxter told me to meet him the following Monday at 10 a.m. in a city park northwest of Los Angeles. I arrived at the park a few minutes prior to 10 a.m. I sat on a bench for about 10 minutes where I could watch the main entrance. I then began walking around wondering whether he was going to show. By 10:15 a.m. I decided that he had changed his mind and was not going to meet me. Just as I was about to leave, I noticed a small older man making his way to a water fountain where I had been standing only a few moments before. He bent down for a drink of water, wiped his mouth, then walked directly up to me and asked if I were Don Hurley. I told him I was, and he nodded toward the bench I had been sitting on earlier. After sitting down, Baxter went over the rules on the interview once more, and for a second time I agreed.

I began by asking Baxter the normal questions. What type of home life did he have? At what point did he have his first brush with the law? He told me a familiar tale of growing up in a large midwestern city during the twenties and early thirties.

Baxter said his father had walked out on him, his older sister, and alcoholic mother when he was just 13 years old. Baxter took to the streets and began running with a bunch who stole anything that wasn't nailed down.

Nick's first encounter with police came when he was 14. He was caught in a stolen car with two other boys. Because of the lack of supervision at home, he was sent to a reform school for 90 days. Baxter told me they liked to call them industrial schools, but "the bastards never missed an opportunity to beat the crap out of you with a strap or anything else they could get their hands on. When I got out, I went home; only it wasn't ours anymore because the bank got it. My 16-year-old sister ran off with some guy, and my mom was living in some flop house. After spending a week trying to sober her up, I decided I'd better take off, too."

Baxter headed for Chicago by way of a freight train. As the train slowed down in the yard, two railroad "dicks" jumped aboard and beat the hell out of him. They took all the money he had, $12, and a pocket knife. After he was finally able to stand up, Baxter headed out of the train yard in a westerly direction. He was hungry when he walked into an automobile garage. Baxter said that he walked right up to an old man who was sitting on a car's running board cleaning spark plugs. He told the old man he was hungry and would work for something to eat. The man told Baxter to call him Sam and asked him how old he was. When Baxter said 18, Sam never batted an eye, but asked him if he would like a job keeping the garage clean. He told Baxter that the job was worth two meals a day, a place to sleep on a cot in the office, and five bucks a week. Baxter felt that his life was taking a turn for the better. He had a steady job, and later he found a girlfriend. Baxter told me that the four years he worked at the garage were some of the happiest years of his life. One Friday afternoon while Sam was at the bank, an older boy Baxter knew casually came into the shop and wanted a ride downtown. He told the boy, "You know I don't own a car." The older boy just pointed to a new Buick in the garage and said they would wait till Sam closed and then take the car for a spin downtown.

The boy left and returned after the garage was closed. Baxter said he reluctantly gave the boy the keys, and the two of them drove off into the night. Baxter told me that they had been driving around town for about an hour. He told the boy to slow down and quit running red lights. Baxter said he no sooner got the words out of his mouth when they were stopped by the cops.

In court even Sam said they had stolen the car from the garage, probably to save face with the owner of the car. "They gave me six months in that 'slimepit,' Cook County Jail.

"After I got out this time, I couldn't get a job, so I began bumming around with a couple of guys I had met in the joint. We started knocking over old ladies for their purses and holding up grocery stores with knives."

Baxter told me that the three of them had decided that after two years of this nickel-and-dime stuff, they needed to move on. He said they stole a car and headed for Cleveland. Baxter said they had agreed to hold up a bank.

Baxter told me they had been in Cleveland about three weeks when they decided on a bank. After watching it for a week, they put their plan into action. They parked the car, which now had stolen Ohio plates on it, about a block away with one person in it. Baxter said he and the other entered the bank, each brandishing a pistol they had taken from a hardware store a week earlier. Before they could get any money, a bank guard stepped out from behind a counter and took a shot at the guy who was with Nick. "The guard missed, so my partner grabbed this woman customer to shield our getaway. Once outside, he threw the woman to the pavement, and we both ran like hell for the car." They jumped in and took off, but did not get very far before running into another car while going through a red light.

Baxter told me that everyone in the car was hurt but him. So he got out and ran as fast and as far as he could. He hid out for two days and two nights in an old warehouse until he got so hungry that he decided to chance going to a restaurant. Within 20 minutes two police officers were tapping Baxter on the shoulder. They pulled out a mug shot from Cook County Jail, agreed it was he, and took him to jail.

Baxter said, "Before I knew it I was in federal court, and some son-of-a-bitch lawyer told me to plead guilty. I did, and I got 30 years for bank robbery and transporting a stolen car across a state line. They shipped me off to the 'big time'" (Leavenworth Federal Penitentiary).

He told me that after a few years of staying out of trouble, another con told him that he thought they could escape. So one Friday afternoon the two hid themselves in a large hospital cart full of dirty laundry which was ready to be put on a truck that was leaving the prison. During a last search at the main gate, both of them were discovered. He said that within three months he found himself, with a bunch of other cons, being herded off a boat at Alcatraz.

I asked Baxter what was his first impression of "The Rock." He said, "I thought I had arrived at the last spot on earth, and I knew I would die here. All the things you heard about the place didn't begin to compare to what it was really like."

I asked him to tell me about Alcatraz. He said every new con that arrived in those days got a complete physical, clothes, blankets, a book of rules, and a cell on the "Broadway Flats." After a few days he was taken before this group of big wig "hacks" (prison officials) who checked your "ticket" (prison record and your crimes) to find out what type of work you could do. They told me then that I would have to prove myself and settle into the routine of the prison before I would be considered for a job. Baxter related that after a few more days each inmate was taken before the man himself. He said he was a little uptight about meeting the warden. He told me that when he was brought into the warden's office, he was surprised to find a little old white-haired man sitting behind a desk. The warden began by saying, "I want you to do your sentence one day at a time. Son, if I see you here in my office again, I am afraid it will not be good news for you." He wished me well, and I was returned to my cell. Baxter stopped for a moment and looked at me and said, "You know, that talk with Warden Johnston was the only time anyone ever called me son." For a full 20 seconds Baxter just stared at the ground.

I then asked him about the prison, other inmates, and the officers. He told me that he found doing time on Alcatraz hard for him because it was the same day in and day out. He told me the routine would drive you nuts, and some of them it did. Someone was always watching you. Then there was the cold weather. It seemed like the cell house was as cold as the jungle (prison yard). Most of the other cons were okay. If you minded your own business, so did they. Some of the big names like Capone and "Doc" Barker were either gone, or like Barker, had their brains blown out trying to "hit the bricks," (escape to San Francisco). Baxter related that Karpis scared the shit out of him and could see why they called him "Creepy." He said that "Machine Gun" Kelly was okay, but he was always bragging, although most everyone liked him. He did not know the "bird man," but had heard that he was always in "dog block" or later in the hospital because he was a "wolf" (aggressive homosexual) who had a bad temper. The only time Baxter said he saw Stroud was when they were dragging him down the hall (D Block) to throw him in solitary for fighting in the yard. He told me that he caught a glimpse of Stroud looking down at him. Baxter related that if you kept your mouth shut and did your job, the "hacks" (officers) left you alone. He said there were some young hacks who tried to lean on you once in awhile, but the older ones kept them in their place.

I asked what happened if an inmate got into trouble. Baxter replied., "If a con knew he was going to the 'hole,' he would always put up a fight. You knew you were going to get the crap kicked out of you, so when the first hack came in your cell you always tried to kick him in the nuts. That way you got your licks in first, and it was also a way to keep the respect of the other cons."

I closed the interview by asking Baxter if he had known my father. He told me that he remembered my father as a big, quiet guy who was even-handed with the cons and always seemed fair. Armed with this fairly good opinion Baxter had of my father, I gave Baxter a hypothetical situation. I told him the year was now 1945 and that my father was the only person who stood between him and his complete freedom from "The Rock." What would he do?

Baxter stared straight ahead for a long time. Then he

turned and looked right at me. I could see his eyes narrow, and I thought that I detected a pure sense of hate in them. He finally replied, "I would kill the son-of-a-bitch in a minute."

Baxter caught me by surprise, I must admit that even though I had spent 20 years in law enforcement and thought that I had interviewed just about every type of criminal known to man, I found myself completely at a loss for words by his reply.

Baxter finally left prison in 1965 to go straight after serving several additional years in the California correctional system for various crimes.

I thanked Baxter for the interview. We shared a handshake, and he turned to leave. I stood there watching as this slightly bent over old man walked out of the park. I sat down on the bench and stared at the ground for a long time. I noted that both Baxter and I had spent about the same number of years on Alcatraz Island, but his time there was as different from mine as day and night.

Perhaps the reason his life had been just the opposite from my own was merely an accident of birth or just a time in history.

ALCATRAZ CLOSING RAISES QUESTIONS ON INCARCERATION

With little fanfare Alcatraz Island Federal Penitentiary closed its doors on March 21, 1963, as a keeper of men. For the first time in its 29-year history, a large number of the press corps was allowed on the island to film and record the transfer of the final 28 prisoners to other federal institutions. (See page 45.)

With its closing several questions were raised about this now-removed link in the Bureau of Prison's penal chain.

1. What was the 29-year Alcatraz experience all about? Was it a success?
2. Could there ever be another Alcatraz in this country?

To answer the first part of the first question is simple. During the gangster era of the 1930s, Alcatraz functioned as a place to lodge the high-profile gangsters in a low-profile setting. Later, as this era ended, the prison would serve as a depository for troublemakers from other federal prisons, deeming everything but medical care, clothing, shelter, and food a privilege. With a few exceptions, an inmate who walked the straight and narrow path might qualify to leave the strict confines of "The Rock" for a less restrictive prison. However, if he went astray, he could look forward to a long, hard stay at Alcatraz.

The second question as to whether there could ever be another Alcatraz Island in this country is even easier than the first part of the first question. Yes, in fact there is a federal penitentiary today that operates in a somewhat similar vein as "The Rock." This penitentiary is Marion near the town of Marion in south-central Illinois. Most all of the rules and regulations that were enforced at Alcatraz have been incorporated at Marion.

Therefore, the concept of a maximum-security with minimum-privilege prison continues within the federal prison system. The author believes there will always be that 1 percent of any prison inmate population, that will not accept any form of rehabilitation nor conform to any rules or regulations. The need will always exist to send this type of individual to a prison such as Marion so that those who do have the desire to rehabilitate themselves can be afforded that chance.

Whether or not practices such as total and extended period of lock-down within Marion can withstand today's legal challenges remains to be seen.

So, in answer to the second half of the first question, the author concludes that Alcatraz was a success in that these extreme examples of criminals were isolated from the rest of the nation's inmate population.

WE TAKE ONE LAST LOOK THROUGH YESTERDAY'S WINDOW

The author spent two years researching for this book in numerous libraries, newspaper files, letters to various government agencies, and interviews. By the end of that period he came to some conclusions.

First, it seems there will always be those who reflect on "The Rock" and suggest that it was not as famous for its tough prison standards as it was for the infamous and colorful characters who served time there. As the years pass by and millions of tourists visit this famous prison, it appears that men like Al "Scarface" Capone, Robert "Birdman of Alcatraz" Stroud, and George "Machine Gun" Kelly take on bigger-than-life qualities.

Secondly, the federal prison at Alcatraz reflected a special time in our country's evolution as much as it reflected a specific type of prison in our nation's society.

ALCATRAZ NOW A HIGH POINT FOR TOURISTS

Today, through the National Park Service, I am afforded the opportunity to meet with the ever-growing number of tourists who visit the island each year. It is with pride that I am able to tell visitors of my 11-year childhood on "The Rock," and, along with park rangers, help relate the island's colorful history.

The Golden Gate National Recreation Area, the largest national urban park in the United States, has a vigorous plan to improve the island. This will insure that in the years to come visitors from all parts of the world will be able to see and hear about this famous landmark. As for myself, I will always remember "The Rock" as it was:

ALCATRAZ ISLAND — MAXIMUM SECURITY

EPILOGUE

Not so long ago, I was walking through the cell house on a very busy tourist weekend. As I passed through "Times Square" (north end of cell house) and entered "Seedy Street," corridor just west of the west side of C Block, I stopped for a moment to observe a man standing in front of me. He was shouting for his wife to keep walking up the corridor so he could film her passing by the cells. As I looked to this man's left, I realized that he was standing in front of cell 402. Another man, Joseph Cretzer, stood there some 43 years earlier while he emptied two full clips of automatic gunfire at point blank range into the bodies of seven of nine correctional officer hostages in a rampage of carnage seldom, if ever, seen in a federal prison. A moment later the man's wife joined him, and they were laughing as they walked from the area. Just for a few moments I stood there staring into cells 402 and 403 and whispered a silent prayer. The noise of the cell house quickly brought me back, and I rejoined the world of the present.

TRIBUTE

Never to be forgotten

In memory of those fallen officers who made the supreme sacrifice:

Royal Cline—Killed during an escape attempt, May 23, 1938
Harold Stites—Killed during the Alcatraz riot, May 2-4, 1946
William Miller—Killed during the Alcatraz riot, May 2-4, 1946

Some will always answer the call

"Most men live between heaven and hell — when you are doing time on The Rock, *you are in hell."*

— Alvin Karpis, 1962

THE ALCATRAZ GLOSSARY

Academy – Prison or jail.

Arctic – Solitary confinement or isolation.

B&W – Bread and water.

Bad/Bum Rap – Unfair or long sentence.

Beating/Flapping the gums – Excessive talking.

Broadway Boulevard – Inmate term for aisle between B and C Blocks.

Cold Storage – Solitary confinement.

Con – Inmate.

Croaker – Prison doctor.

Dog Block – Treatment unit or isolation.

Easy Go – Good inmate job.

Flats – Bottom or ground floor cells.

Fresh Fish – Newly arrived inmate.

Gas Chamber – Name given to dining room because of gas canisters attached to ceiling.

General Population – Inmates housed in B and C Blocks.

The Green Carpet – Prison disciplinary board hearing.

Gun Bull – Armed officer.

Hack – Common inmate term for correctional officer.

Head Screw – Warden.

Hole/Hot Box – Terms for solitary confinement.

House – Inmate term for his cell.

Jailbird – Inmate doing a long sentence.

Jungle – Prison yard.

Kite – Illegal notes passed among inmates.

Michigan Boulevard – Inmate term for aisle between A and B Blocks.

Monkey Suit – Officer's uniform.

Pig Sticker – Knife.

Rack – Manual mechanism to open or close cell door.

Rain Check – Parole.

SallyPort – Controlled inmate entrance or exit point.

Screw – Officer.

Screw Driver – Captain.

Seedy Street – Inmate term for aisle between C and D Blocks.

Shooting Gallery – East or west gun gallery.

Ticket – Inmate's record or discipline report.

Track "13" – Life sentence.

Wolf – An aggressive homosexual.

BIBLIOGRAPHY

BOOKS

Campbell, Bruce J., *A Farewell to the Rock, Escape from Alcatraz*, McGraw-Hill Book Company, New York, 1963.

Clark, Howard, *Six Against the Rock*, A Jova HB Book, New York, 1977.

De Nevi, Don, and Phillip Bergen, *Alcatraz '46, The Anatomy of a Classic Prison Tragedy*, Leswing Press, San Rafael, 1974.

Denis, Alherra, *Spanish Alta California*, MacMillan, 1927.

Heaney, Frank and Guy Machado, *Inside the Walls of Alcatraz*, Bull Publishing Company, Palo Alto,1987.

Johnston, James A., *Alcatraz Island Prison—And the Men Who Live There*, Charles Scribner's, New York, 1949.

Lewis, Emanuel Raymond, *Seacoast Fortification of the United States: An Introductory History*, Smithsonian Institute Press, Washington, 1970.

Nash, Robert Jay, *Bloodletters and Badmen: A Narrative Encyclopedia of American Criminals*, Evansand Co., New York, 1973.

Odier, Pierre, *The Rock—A History of Alcatraz, The Fort/The Prison*, L'Image Odier, Eagle Rock, 1982.

Shanks, Ralph C., Jr., *Lighthouse of San Francisco Bay*, Costano Books, San Anselmo, 1976.

Who Discovered San Francisco Bay? San Mateo County Historical Association, 1966.

FOR ADDITIONAL BOOKS:
Send check or money order for

ALCATRAZ ISLAND—MAXIMUM SECURITY................. $10.95

ALCATRAZ ISLAND MEMORIES...................................... $ 8.95

Plus shipping/packaging for either book at $3.00 total.
Order TWO or more of either book, and we pay ALL postage.

To Order:

Fog Bell Enterprises
P.O. Box 1376
Sonoma, CA 95476

One or both books make a great gift.